DesignArt

Alex Coles

DesignArt

On art's romance with design

Tate Publishing

Acknowledgements

For Sophie

First published 2005 by order of the Tate Trustees by Tate Publishing, a division of Tate Enterprises Ltd, Millbank, London SW1P 4RG www.tate.org.uk/publishing

© Tate 2005

British Library Cataloguing in Publication Data A catalogue record for this book is available from the British Library

ISBN 1-85437-520-2

Distributed in the United States and Canada by Harry N. Abrams, Inc., New York

Library of Congress Cataloging in Publication Data Library of Congress Control Number: 2004114447

Designed by 01.02 Printed in Hong Kong by Printing Express Limited

This book started life in numerous articles and papers. Thanks therefore to the editors at *Art Monthly*, *Contemporary*, *Frieze*, *Parachute* and *Design Issues*. Thanks, too, to those who invited me to lecture on the subject – in the UK at the Royal College of Art and the Bartlett School of Architecture, and in the US at Cranbrook School of Art and Design in Michigan and Maine College of Art and Design in Portland.

For their support and advice I would like to thank David Batchelor, David Blamey, Cornelia Grassi, Jorge Pardo, Sandra Percival, Christiane Schneider and especially Barry Schwabsky. Thanks are also due to those involved with the editing, production and design of the book: Nicola Bion, Adam Brown, Clare Manchester, Emma Woodiwiss and Roger Thorp.

Finally, I am grateful to Surrey Institute of Art and Design for a grant to assist with production costs.

Cover: Takashi Murakami, *LV Monolith* 2003 (detail)
(see also pp.32–4)
Courtesy Marianne Boesky Gallery, New York/Louis Vuitton
Frontispiece: Dave Muller, *Supergraphic* 1999 (detail),
Courtesy Blum & Poe, Los Angeles
p.6: Donald Judd, *Untitled* 1993 (detail)
p.20: Emilio Pucci, Women modelling Pucci clothes 1969 (detail)
p.48: Charlotte Perriand, Jean Prouvé and Sonia Delaunay,
Shelves/Room Divider 1953 (detail)
p.72: Richard Hamilton with Lawrence Alloway and Victor
Pasmore, *An exhibit* 1957 (detail)
p.100: Richard Neutra, Kaufman House 1946 (detail)
p.132: Pae White, Magazine advertisement for gallery
neugerriemschneider 2001 (detail)

Contents

Introduction

Some people like to just gaze at art, others like to sit on it. To a large extent it depends on what kind of art it is and what you want to get out of it. Of course, both approaches are valid, but in a way this book is about the type of art that you can look at while you are sitting on it.

It may sound simple, but since there has always been a rift between these two very different ways of encountering things, it obviously is not. Purists submit that the distance between art and design has to be preserved in the name of specificity; in an age where there is a multimedia meltdown, they warn that art must take care not to relinquish what is specific to it. Meanwhile, more nonchalant players insist that, on the contrary, to survive and be relevant in such an age art needs to be more gregarious – it must reach out beyond its own confines – and design is surely one of its more suitable bedfellows. The sense of specificity that comes with an awareness of a discipline's history is, however, as important to designart as the ability to make connections between disciplines. So perhaps both groups are partially misguided.

Project 2000, a recent installation by Jorge Pardo (b. 1963) at Dia:Chelsea in New York, is a good example of why a comprehensive knowledge of the different disciplines is important. Pardo refashioned Dia:Chelsea's ground-floor gallery, bookstore and lobby in such a way that integrated these three formerly discrete areas into a flowing stream of vibrant tiles. To experience the installation was thus to be catapulted into a vertiginous world enveloping both the art gazer and book buyer alike. By way of reprieve, pastel-coloured murals also conceived by Pardo occupied both ends of

the space, and an adjacent office area was filled with his low-hanging lamps. A full-scale clay model of Volkswagen's most recent Beetle took centre stage in the gallery, while in the bookshop there was a seating area replete with delicately arranged chairs designed by Marcel Breuer (1902–81) and Alvar Aalto (1898–1976) in the 1920s and 1930s. Pardo effectively preserved a sense of specificity in the installation through the decisive articulation of each space and object, while at the same time striving to be gregarious by drawing the objects that constituted the installation from across art and design.

Such installations have rendered design crucial to an understanding of contemporary art. So, too, have the flurry of recent group exhibitions devoted to designart. These include *What If? Art on the Verge of Architecture and Design*, at the Moderna Museet in Stockholm, 2000; *Against Design*, at the Institute for Contemporary Art, University of Pennsylvania, Philadelphia, 2000; *Beau-Monde: Toward a Redeemed Cosmopolitanism*, Site Santa Fe, 2001–2; and *Trespassing: Houses x Artists* at the MAK Center for Art and Architecture, Los Angeles, 2003. Despite these exhibitions, extended critical commentaries on the trend have been noticeably lacking.

Vilém Flusser (1920–91), the philosopher and witty commentator on design, devoted an entire essay to a simple explanation of the etymology of the word. 'The word is derived from the Latin *signum*, meaning sign, and shares the same ancient root. Thus, etymologically, *design* means de-sign.'[1] Flusser subsequently elaborated on other words used in the same context, such as 'technology'. 'The Greek word

Jorge Pardo
Project
2000
Installation at Dia:
Chelsea, New York

techne means art and is related to *tekton*, a carpenter. The basic idea here is that wood is a shapeless material to which the artist, the technician, gives form, thereby causing the form to appear in the first place.'[2] In this account the words 'design', 'machine', 'technology' and 'art' are closely related, one term being unthinkable without the others. But modern bourgeois culture of the mid-nineteenth century made a sharp distinction between the world of the arts and that of technology, and as a result culture has been split into two mutually exclusive branches: one scientific, quantifiable and 'hard', the other aesthetic, evaluative and 'soft'. This unfortunate split became irreversible

towards the end of the nineteenth century, and in the end the word design came to form a bridge between the two. In Flusser's late twentieth-century reading, design indicates the site where art and technology meet to produce new forms of culture, and so the role that design plays is crucial to the vitality of the arts.

But artists and critics have had a field day denying the impact of design on art. Intrepid formalists from Roger Fry to Michael Fried have tended to foreground what they termed the 'design' of a work, while at the same time paradoxically playing down the design context – tricky, given that much of what they support comes from a narrow reading of the 1920s Bauhaus school. For them, design is a structure that can carry the artist's aesthetic conviction; in no way is it respectable in itself. Conceptual artists of the late 1960s tended likewise to be evasive about design, with the result that many of their arguments also appear weak, especially considering their substantial recourse to industrial design and typography – the role of typography in the work of Art & Language, for example, just being the tip of the iceberg. To the extent that without design the work of both formalists and Conceptual artists is inconceivable, it seems unfair that they refer to it in a pejorative sense. A key issue to keep in mind while thinking through designart is that all art is designed even if it endeavours to appear otherwise. In the end, then, for artists it is really just a matter of emphasis: to be overt or covert about an engagement with design. Of those artists to approach design, only the Pop artists fully embraced it: Richard Artschwager (b. 1923) is open about starting out as a furniture maker, Andy Warhol (1928–89) did not hide that

Jorge Pardo
Project
2000
Installation at
Dia:Chelsea, New York
Volkswagen New Beetle
Full-Scale Model 1995
Collection: Volkswagen
Design, Simi Valley
CA and Wolfsburg

Ed Ruscha
*Surrealism soaped
and scrubbed*
Cover for *Artforum*,
September 1996

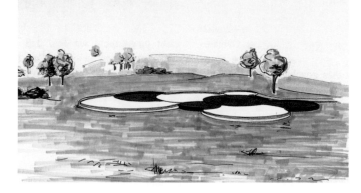

Tobias Rehberger
Drawing for the planned parking place installation 1997
Courtesy neugerriemschneider, Berlin

he had previously been an illustrator and the London-based Independent Group (1952–5) went so far as to include designers and architects among their kind. Even within Pop there were some misgivings though: Ed Ruscha (b. 1937) published his graphic design work from the mid-1960s under the name of Eddie Russia, a pun on the political climate of the time, to be sure, but also on art's fear of design.

More exhilarating still was the Minimalists' strategic coyness towards design. In the 1980s Donald Judd (1928–93) ordered chairs and tables to be fabricated according to his specifications. Even though they were eminently close in tone to the sculptures he had been producing since the early 1960s – sleek in structure, deadpan in facture – Judd endeavoured to keep the two strands of his output distinct. So anxious was he about this divide and what it meant that he took great care to protect his double life. While hours were spent scheming away behind the scenes, Don the designer was rarely seen in public with Judd the artist, as he foresaw this could lead to all his output being exclusively contextualised within the design world. The consequence of this would surely have been that his occasional forays into *Home and Garden* territory on art and its relation to the interior would be taken as the cornerstone of his theoretical output, undesirable for a philosophy graduate accustomed to writing for *Artforum*. After all, Judd is an artist who occasionally turned his hand to design when he needed something to sit on, eat off or live in – or simply to make money from. According to Judd himself, he was in no way a designer *per se*.

To a more recent generation of artists, while it has the look of design, Judd's work does not implement any of the characteristics they associate with it, such as an open attitude towards working with different disciplines or the ambition to create conditions for the viewer to have a truly dialogistic experience. With this idea in mind Tobias Rehberger (b. 1966) recently suggested that one of Judd's outdoor sculptures be temporarily refashioned into a bar in order to produce a new collaborative artwork. The Judd Foundation turned the proposition down flat. Explaining the motivation behind projects such as Rehberger's, Liam Gillick (b. 1964), had this to say: 'in common with many people of my generation I embraced certain aspects of design as a part of a critique of established terms of judgement within an art context'.[3] In the eyes of this generation of artists, Judd is no longer able to hold himself aloof from the design context.

But in the parlance of Judd's time, the problem with Gillick's spin on design and Rehberger's proposal is that a piece of high art would be turned into that much-maligned thing: good design. The term 'good design' actually derives from an annual exhibition of contemporary design trends mounted by The Museum of Modern Art, New York (MoMA), between the late 1940s and the mid-1950s in the hope that something of their aesthetic would make its way into the culture at large.

Designer and theorist George Nelson (1907–86) furnished an account of what good design looked like during this period, with particular reference to what he termed the 'plywood and rubber plant school of good design'.[4] With his tongue firmly in cheek, Nelson recounted how an

Donald Judd
Untitled
1993
Courtesy PaceWildenstein, New York

architect of his acquaintance had bought a station wagon because he had recently designed a number of modern houses that were to be published in the architectural press. Since his clients owned no modern furniture, in order to achieve the required interior shots the architect was forced to load the station wagon with a photographer, his cameras and lights, a large rubber plant and a few Aalto stools, armchairs and tables. Nelson's story reveals how ubiquitous the notion of 'good design' had become by the mid-1950s, and hence almost meaningless to cutting-edge designers and artists like himself. Given this levelling-out of cultural territory, it makes sense that the term was often used by art critics seeking to disparage new art forms they considered too smooth for their gritty avant-garde tastes. For example, in the late 1960s Clement Greenberg (1909–94) observed that he felt 'back in the realm of Good Design' when in the presence of Minimalist work.[5] By the same token, a few lines later he also suggested that painters like Ellsworth Kelly (b. 1923) and Kenneth Noland (b. 1924) set an example to be followed as they 'rise above Good Design' while utilising formal elements derived from design, particularly the Bauhaus. Although all this was years ago, still it came as no surprise, when the most recent designart came to the attention of critics in the late 1990s, that the same terminology was served up again. According to some critics and artists from previous generations, especially the ones still under the influence of Judd's generation, Pardo's work nestles comfortably within the confines of good design. And so once again the high art of one generation is seen as the good design of another.

The term 'designart' only adds to the furore. Perhaps it erodes the ideological gulf between the disciplines too smoothly. Let it be clear from the outset then that it is a term derived from many of the contemporary artists associated with it. Joe Scanlan (b. 1961) for one frequently peppers his felicitous essays on the subject with it. Here he is in 2001 in an essay co-authored with Neal Jackson (b. 1959) entitled 'Please, Eat the Daisies', furnishing the reader with a crisp explanation of the term: 'Design art could be defined loosely as any artwork that attempts to play with the place, function and style of art by commingling it with architecture, furniture and graphic design.'[6] The active development and use of the term 'designart' by artists sharply differentiates it from, say, Minimalism, a term its alleged exponents were none too happy with, as it was applied to their work by an external body, the critic. Sometimes the two words – 'design' and 'art' – are kept apart by artists, but just as frequently they are run together. In print this appears to make a difference, but in actual fact it is only a semantic one and is not visible in their work. So there is no need to get too bound up in the term itself.

Most often when designart is discussed it is in terms of the way it 'transgresses' boundaries. But making too much of this particular issue is to befuddle an already complicated situation. For it is not so much that these artists transgress boundaries, as that they engage art and design in a romance which is of interest. The notion of 'simultaneity' is useful here because the most enticing design artists are utterly flexible regarding the role they play, being content to work as designers and as artists at different times, although not always in the role or circumstances in which they would be expected to do so. Sonia Delaunay (1884–1979) was the first to use the term in the 1920s. Perceiving the practices of certain artists from her time onwards as simultaneous alleviates the necessity to think of designart as a fixed paradigm or movement.

The economy of the exchange between art and design is also worth considering. To artists, design is attractive because it provides a way to make money, to reach a larger audience, to look stylish – not to mention having something to sit on and live in while you are making more designart. Art entices designers as it is something you can acquire attitude from if you want to appear profound while at the same time producing something to go on your wall. Numerous members of the current group of design artists, many of whom grew up in the early 1970s, have their own version of the economy of this exchange between art and design. Scanlan's is particularly judicious: 'I think most of the design artists want to be the chill out kids in *The Ice Storm* ([Ang Lee, 1997] great movie), but we aren't cool enough. We are not Gavin Brown or Rirkrit [Tiravanija], or even Christina Ritchie or Toby McGuire. We are the dark little brother who has the hots for Christina but is conflicted about it: an unfulfilled and terrifying desire.'[7]

DesignArt unapologetically focuses on a select group of artists who have either been receptive to or worked with design, rather than focusing on designers *per se*. To this end, the key themes running through the book revolve around what each artist uses design for: whether it is simply to achieve a more rigorous composition; to play disciplines off one another in a creative show-down; to gain control over the various elements that represent them, such as exhibition catalogues, that are so often left to designers; or to produce a new speculative type of work truly somewhere in-between art and design. A debate over the actual nature of the liaison that the meeting between art and design yields soon follows these considerations. Is the meeting part and parcel of a revolutionary gusto to change the way we live according to an ideological doxy? Does it regard just bathing every part of an individual's life in opulent decoration? Or is the meeting to do with gently nurturing new ways of living in and around art and design that are as yet unknown through continual experimentation?

Many of these considerations turn on the way in which ornament and decoration relate to designart and are often naively opposed to utility. Since the infamous essay, 'Ornament and Crime', written by Adolf Loos (1870–1933) in 1908, there has been a tendency to assume that ornament, and with it the decorative effects of art, architecture and design, are degenerate or are at the very least superfluous to what is required. In Loos's account these effects were a product of the way in which exponents of the Art Nouveau style at the turn of the twentieth century tended to run the different disciplines together. Loos made a moral imperative out of his theory that disciplines must be kept apart in order to limit the decorative: 'I have discovered the following truth and present it to the world: cultural evolution is equivalent to the removal of ornament from articles in daily use.'[8] Not satisfied with stopping there with his drive to expunge ornament from his life, Loos even subjected his diet to the same relentless discipline:

'The spectacular menus of past centuries, which all include decorations to make peacocks, pheasants and lobsters appear even tastier, produce the opposite effect on me. I walk through a culinary display with revulsion at the thought that I am supposed to eat these stuffed animal corpses. I eat roast beef.'[9] Today this tendency continues. In *Design and Crime (and Other Diatribes)*, 2002, Hal Foster bemoans the loss of specificity in the name of Loos's polemic against ornament. Loos's 'anti-decorative dictate is a modernist mantra if ever there was one', Foster asserts, 'and it is for the puritanical propriety inscribed in such words that postmodernists have condemned modernists like Loos in turn'.[10] Foster perceives that times have changed again, since 'maybe we are in a moment when distinctions between practices might be reclaimed or re-made'.[11] The notion of specificity is played off against the tendency to work across disciplines and

on this occasion specificity once again wins. So it is not difficult to understand from the remainder of the book that Foster takes things even further than Loos by clinging to a strict vegetarian-like diet of medium-specific art.

As a repercussion of how the terms of Loos's inquiry continue to dominate the entire debate, there is a necessity to recover the discourse about forms of design that accent the ornamental and decorative. It is no coincidence that this task is at the very centre of the texts of some of the most unfashionably incisive critics who have written about the correspondence between art and design: John Ruskin (1819–1900), William Morris (1834–96) and Oscar Wilde (1854–1900). The first two promoted a social agenda that was bound up with the aesthetic effects of ornamentation. Making a case for handcrafted design, they perceived that the divisions made between the arts of the 'intellect' – architecture, sculpture

Kenneth Price
(foreground)
Underhung 1997
Ellsworth Kelly
(background)
Blue Black Red Green
2000
Oil on canvas, four panels
254 × 1229.4cm
Santa Fe 4th International
Biennial July 2001 –
January 2002

and painting – and those of the 'decorative' – interior architecture, the crafts – were based on a false presupposition. In his essay 'The Lesser Arts', signed off in 1882, Morris asserted that his agenda was to study the subject that is the 'great body of art, by means of which men have at all times more or less striven to beautify the familiar matters of everyday life'.[12] Ruskin likewise insisted in 1859 that:

there is no existing highest-order for art but is decorative. The best sculpture yet produced has been the decoration of a temple front – the best painting, the decoration of a room ... Get rid, then, at once of any idea of Decorative art being a degraded or a separate kind of art.[13]

Wilde concurred with their insights but skewed their methodologies to such an extent that his version charged that the frivolity that ornament encouraged could, at its most superlative, be transgressive; he alone elucidated how sensual freedom could ride on the back of an aesthetic flourish. *The Picture of Dorian Gray*, published in 1891, advocates such aesthetic reverie, and nowhere more effectively than in the opening scene:

From the corner of the divan of Persian saddle-bags on which he was lying, smoking, as was his custom, innumerable cigarettes, Lord Henry Wotton could just catch the gleam of the honey-sweet and honey-coloured blossoms of a laburnum ... and now and then the fantastic shadows of birds in flight flitted across the long tussore-silk curtains that were stretched in front of the huge window, producing a kind of momentary Japanese effect ... In the centre of the room, clamped to an upright easel, stood the full-length portrait of a young man of extraordinary personal beauty.[14]

Wilde pans across myriad disciplines –

including contemporary interior decoration, Japanese ornament and avant-garde painting – in one eloquent swoop. Since his critical essays on decoration and craft rest on a similar undertaking, there will be recourse to draw on them later on.

The critics mentioned above were loosely associated with the Arts and Crafts movement in Britain in the late nineteenth century. In numerous ways the so-called great avant-gardes that followed in the early twentieth century – De Stijl in the Netherlands, the Bauhaus in Germany and the Russian Constructivists – forwarded theories sympathetic to the art and design issue. But writings by the exponents of these movements pursued a much more exacting sense of how correlations between art and design could be pressed into service by utilising a muscular theoretical programme. In 'The Theory and Organisation of the Bauhaus' from 1923, Walter Gropius (1883–1969) asserted that, 'The Bauhaus strives to co-ordinate all creative effort, to achieve ... the unification of all training in art and design. The ultimate, if distant, goal of the Bauhaus is the collective work of art ... in which no barriers exist between the structural and the decorative arts.'[15] As a result of Gropius's characteristically firm purchase on the situation, the flexibility and frivolity that Wilde's prose exhumes is limited. Decorative effects are discarded and the kinks are straightened out. Gropius's discourse allowed the avant-garde's aim of bringing the arts together, but the sense of flexibility that such a meeting ought to yield is forfeited – the running together of the arts became a dry theoretical programme almost as disagreeable as Loos's. As a result of the

1 Vilém Flusser, 'About the Word *Design*', *The Shape of Things: A Philosophy of Design*, London and New York 1999, p.17.
2 Ibid.
3 Liam Gillick, 'The Semiotics of the Built World', *Liam Gillick: The Woodway*, exh. cat., Whitechapel Art Gallery, London 2002, p.81.
4 George Nelson, 'Modern Decoration', *George Nelson on Design*, London 1979, p.185.
5 Clement Greenberg, 'Recentness of Sculpture' (1967), *Clement Greenberg: The Collected Essays and Criticism*, ed. John O' Brian, vol.4, Chicago and London 1993, p.254.
6 Joe Scanlan and Neal Jackson, 'Please, Eat the Daisies', *Art Issues*, January/February 2001, p.26.
7 Scanlan, private correspondence with the author, summer 2003.
8 Adolf Loos, 'Ornament and Crime' (1908), *Programs and Manifestoes on Twentieth-Century Architecture*, ed. Ulrich Conrads, Cambridge, Massachsetts, 1964, p.20.
9 Ibid., p.21.

10 Hal Foster, *Design and Crime (and Other Diatribes)*, London and New York 2002, p.14.
11 Ibid.
12 William Morris, 'The Lesser Arts' (1882), *Art in Theory: 1815–1900*, ed. Charles Harrison, William Wood and Jason Geiger, Cambridge, Massachusetts, and London 1998, p.751.
13 John Ruskin, 'The Decorative Arts' (1859), *The Two Paths*, London 1956, pp.74–6.
14 Oscar Wilde, *The Picture of Dorian Gray* (1891), London and New York 2000, p.7.
15 Walter Gropius, 'The Theory and Organisation of the Bauhaus' (1923), *Art in Theory 1900–1990*, ed. Charles Harrison and William Wood, Cambridge, Massachusetts, and London 1993, p.340.
16 Henri Matisse, 'Notes of a Painter' (1908), *Matisse on Art*, ed. Jack Flam, revised ed., Berkeley 2001, p.42.

widespread dissemination of Bauhaus dogma, especially in the United States the speculative aspects of design and decoration were hampered, if not embarrassed, into silence until the mid-1950s, when the likes of the Independent Group returned to the issue anew. The dialogue did indeed flourish in the 1960s, as the chapters below attest, but it was superseded by slices of grey neo-Conceptualism right through to the mid-1990s when these issues once again came under the spotlight of critical attention through the exhibitions mentioned earlier. This brings us up-to-date.

By responding to the questions posed above, *DesignArt* presses for a more flexible approach towards design. Recovering discourses such as Wilde's on ornament is part and parcel of this project. So too is the recovery of the work of artists such as Henri Matisse (1869–1954). For it is no coincidence that Matisse is one of the few artists making a walk on appearance in almost every one of the chapters that follow, from the easel paintings in the first chapter on pattern, to the inclusion of his Chapel of the Rosary in Vence in the final one devoted to architecture. Matisse's insouciant attitude towards design was noticeably far more speculative in nature than that of either the Bauhaus or Loos, who both strove for mastery over it. Matisse's work is malleable enough to take inspiration from border disciplines and yet strong enough to stimulate them in return. He always ensured that rather than disappearing, boundaries between disciplines were only momentarily blurred. And it is precisely this emphasis on the transitory – that is, on the permeable, over the solidly defined or conversely the completely erased –

border, that gives Matisse's art its potency today. It is thus also fitting that Matisse should have the last word in this introduction with a statement from 1908 – the same year as Loos's diatribe against ornament – that ingeniously turns a painting into a piece of design without even sweating:

What I dream of is an art of balance, of purity and serenity, devoid of troubling or depressing subject matter, an art that could be for every mental worker, for the businessman as well as the man of letters, for example, a soothing, calming influence on the mind, something like a good armchair that provides relaxation from fatigue.[16]

Henri Matisse
The Window
1916
The Detroit
Institute of Arts.
City of Detroit Purchase

Pattern

1

Pattern

Since Henri Matisse first began transforming interiors bathed in ambrosial colour into his own unique brand of chromatic carpentry, the charge that abstract painting is mere decoration has been continuously levelled at it. Clearly this is because Aldof Loos's rhetoric continued through a good portion of modernist criticism, not an unexpected occurrence in view of how slim the discourse available on ornament was. For example, the writing on ornamental Romanesque art by the art historian Alois Riegl (1858–1905) from the end of the nineteenth century, was not viewed as being relevant by the Bauhaus generation and in addition was not translated from German until quite recently. And when the subject of ornament was taken up in the latter half of the twentieth century by the popular art historian Ernst Gombrich in his almost scientific book, *A Sense of Order* (1979), the results were notable only for lacking the felicity of his Austrian forebear. While it is not surprising, it is unfortunate that today many are still in accord with the modernist critics descending from the Bauhaus who suggested that wild pattern was frivolous. For just because an artist uses pattern it does not necessarily mean that they are making a play for the marketplace, although of course it can do.

Often used to counter the abundance and insipid character of much wallpaper design, abstract painting soon took over its function, especially in the contexts of collectors' habitats and their corporate premises – above the fireplace and in the lobby, respectively, being the favoured quarters. The tendency of abstract painting to be decorative was augmented to such an extent, that by the 1950s abstract painters such as Ellsworth Kelly and Kenneth Noland used motifs far more complex than those splayed across the wallpaper then in vogue. Today, contemporary artists whose work is part of the ongoing development of pattern, such as Takashi Murakami (b. 1962) and Tobias Rehberger, are so attentive to the possible co-adoption of their work to decorative ends that often they premise their work precisely on this being inevitable. The upshot is a tight reciprocity between painting and textile design.

Painters have taken up the decorative in numerous ways, but it was Matisse who piloted the viability of a flexible relationship with design: 'The decorative for a work of art is an extremely precious thing. It is an essential quality. It is not pejorative to say that the paintings of an artist are decorative.'[1] Matisse's *Interior with Aubergines* from 1911 provides a clear example of how the subject can be judiciously dealt with by making decoration the subject of a painting without the painting forfeiting its own decorative function. To this end the painting establishes a background surface constituted by an ultramarine and mahogany flower-print motif on which everything else floats; surprisingly, considering the way in which it is punctuated by the planes that follow, this layer actually covers the entire painting. The next plane consists of a screen covered with a strong curvilinear pattern that hugs the middle of the composition. The next one again is a rectangular section of flowery wallpaper that serves as a backdrop to a still life, the crowning glory of which are the aubergines. Surface juxtaposes surface in this interplay of pattern to such an extent that some

Henri Matisse
Interior with Aubergines
1911
Musée de Grenoble

strange things happen. So vertiginous are the decorative effects, that for a moment the first plane appears to come forwards as if it was about to envelop the still life, before it suddenly snaps back into place again.

Throughout the 1920s and 1930s, once his reputation was secured, Matisse conceived a number of designs for rugs, neckerchiefs, screens and tapestries, in close correspondence with his paintings. He also designed numerous ballet costumes, the first for *Le chant du rossignol* 1919–20, by Sergei Diaghilev (1872–1929), the second for *Rouge et Noir* 1939, by Léonid Massine (1896–1979). The costumes realised in three dimensions the compositions that Matisse depicted in the fictive depth of the picture plane. For example, *Costume for a Mourner*, a cotton and felt robe replete with triangles and stripes cut out of silk and velvet commissioned for *Le chant du rossignol*, looks as if it has been wrenched from the screen depicted in *Interior with Aubergines*. The simplicity of the costume's fabrication found its way into the artist's cut-out technique in the 1940s, in which sheets of coloured paper were cut out and pasted onto heavier paper. This technique was fully realised in a book project Matisse started in 1943 entitled *Jazz*. The works that ensued signalled a decorative height of sorts for the artist and yet resisted becoming too sedate due to the precise manner in which his previous tendency to orchestrate colours harmonically was replaced by a keen propensity to compose them according to the cacophonous beat of jazz. For instance, the regulated red and orange squares constituting the back plane of *Creole Dancer* (1947) are suddenly ripped through at an angle, bebop-like, by the

ecstatic figure of a dancer rendered in lurid green. At the same time as creating such stand-alone cut outs in the early 1950s, Matisse turned this process to the composition of vestments to be worn by the priests in the Chapel of the Rosary in Vence. The relationship between Matisse's paintings and his design work thus turns on a carefully studied simultaneity throughout the various stages of his development.

Sonia Delauney was the first to truly co-ordinate her paintings with fabric and clothes design. These ideas were unthinkable without Matisse's example, as she attests in her 1926 essay, 'The Influence of Painting on Fashion Design': 'Matisse took up the task [of] rendering the relations of colours sharper – in effect exacerbating them. This exacerbation of colour concluded by deforming and breaking the line. He even … tried to achieve the effect of objects … on the surface plane, like a poster.'[2] Delaunay's paintings were derivative of other Parisian avant-garde painters until 1911, when she designed a quilt cover for her son. The quilt has a semblance of the collage technique, usually considered as not being introduced until a year later by the Cubists, but the methods behind its composition are in fact quite distinct. For rather than a figurative subject, the point of departure for assembling the quilt was a compositional process that entailed the placement of a single patch of colour that then determined the size, shape and placement of its neighbour until a harmonic arrangement was achieved. Even though they were not started until a year later than the quilt, both Delaunay's abstract paintings and her dresses clearly have their conceptual origin here.

Sonia Delaunay
*Embroidered coat
for Gloria Swanson*
1923

Sonia Delaunay
(opposite)
Expo 1925,
models with car 1925

Developed concurrently with the textiles, Delaunay's paintings of this period are experiments in unbridled form and colour. By 1914 she began incorporating text and collage elements drawn from the quotidian signage of advertisements into her paintings. Many of her paintings from this period toy with pure abstraction and develop what eventually became a predilection for crisp linear forms executed in blazing colours, elements clearly evident in a series entitled *Discs* from 1916. The disc is such a pivotal element in Delaunay's paintings because of the way it can be used to inject motion into a stable, fixed plane. In some of her compositions it even appears as if the discs spin only in order to be steadied by the rectangular elements. By 1917 the understanding she had garnered from abstract painting was of a sufficient depth to allow her to make the full leap into textiles.

A year prior to Matisse's first costume commission in 1918, Delaunay was invited to contribute the costumes to Diaghilev's re-staging of *Cleopatra*. Delaunay experimented with designs of lengths of fabric to be wrapped around the human form in the garment for the lead character; she also designed a costume for another character, an intricate arrangement of discs of sunlit colours defined by rings of sequins and pearls. The commission was a success, as were the hand-made dresses she began making at the same time. Delaunay thus resolved to begin producing printed textiles, an activity that required its very own workshop. With their contrasts of vividly coloured geometrical forms, her vibrant fabrics adorned key figures of the Jazz Age. Gloria Swanson's embroidered wool coat tailored by Delaunay in 1923

is fitting attire for one of the most glamorous movie stars of the period, and its composition of a series of interlocking rectangular forms makes the fabric appear to move in tempo with its wearer. The term Delaunay coined to refer to her innovation was 'simultaneous fabric' – apt, considering that they were the first fabrics to be conceived in relation to the actual garments they were intended to be made into:

At present, fashion has become constructive, clearly influenced by painting. The construction and cut of the dress is henceforth to be conceived at the same time as its decoration ... It is the fabric pattern. The cut of the dress is conceived by its creator simultaneously with its decoration. Afterward, the cut and decoration appropriate to the form is printed on the same fabric. The result is the first collaboration between the creator of the model and the creator of the fabric.[3]

The 'simultaneous fabrics' were so successful that the bohemian novelist Colette (1873–1954) gushed in *Vogue*: 'But short, flat, geometrical, rectangular women's clothing took the parallelogram as its template, and 1925 will not welcome the return of a fashion of soft curves, a proud breast, succulent hips.'[4] In 1925 Delaunay painted the bodywork of a dashing Citroën B12, a car considered the height of urban chic at the time. The pattern deployed on the car consists of a series of interlocking rectangles of various hues and tones that are truly at odds with the traditional monochrome surface covering most cars. Her decorative scheme breaks the surface up into a series of rhythms, which in turn bounce off those patterned across the coats and headscarves she also designed for the similarly fashionable driver. Rather than appearing to be an addition to the car,

Emilio Pucci
Women modelling clothes on the top of Palazzo Pucci, Florence 1969

Delaunay's pattern is perfectly in unison with its sleek design – as if it had been a characteristic of it from the very first. In 1967 Delaunay applied the same process to the Matra B530 sports car with equally enticing results. While the Citroën was eye catching, the Mantra is even more so, partly because by this time car design had caught up with the avant-garde's penchant for sleek contours rendered in highly exaggerated hues. Recently, Tobias Rehberger has even fashioned his very own car, a lemon yellow Porche 911 (*nana* 2000).

The notion of simultaneity at work in Delaunay's individual fabrics also extends to the way in which she conceived of her practice. When in 1924 she decided to produce her first printed fabrics, the following note was boldly run along the edges: 'Sonia Delaunay – Atelier simultané', affirming her wish not to dissociate her decorative work from her paintings. Delaunay's working studies for the fabrics actually have the feel of finished paintings although they could double as either wallpaper or fabric designs. They anticipate the aesthetic of the sportswear designed by Emilio Pucci (1914–92) in the 1950s and also the predilection in the 1960s for paintings with rigorous geometric lines bursting with optical intensity, realised in the work of Bridget Riley (b. 1931) and Frank Stella (b. 1936). Delaunay's *Stripes*, a gouache dated 1925, is a case in point, and consists of a dozen or so bands, each a slightly different width, their colours moving from cold to hot, as black and burnt sienna give way to cadmium red and lemon yellow. The work emanates a sense of playfulness that is current throughout the artist's oeuvre. At the same time, this gouache also clarifies how her work addresses an underlying inquiry: to reconsider the avant-garde's relationship to the mainstream. For Delaunay piloted a way for the avant-garde to encapsulate the mainstream, and for the mainstream in turn to encompass the avant-garde. In a way she rounded-out the hard edges of the avant-garde. Hence, while Delaunay distanced herself from the superfluous mainstream excesses of Art Deco, the visual style of the Jazz Age, she contributed her own understanding of it from within the avant-garde – a further simultaneity of sorts. As if to confound this, if Colette thought Delaunay a fit subject, so did the avant-garde poet Guillaume Apollinaire (1880–1918):

Here is a description of one of Mme Sonia Delaunay's simultaneous dresses: purple dress, wide purple and green belt, and under the jacket, a corsage divided into brightly colored zones, delicate or faded where the following colors are mixed: antique rose, yellow-orange, nattier blue, scarlet, etc., appearing on different materials, so that woolen cloth, taffeta, tulle, flannelette, watered silk, and *peau de soie* are juxtaposed. So much variety cannot escape notice. It transforms fantasy into elegance.[5]

It is as if Apollinaire also understood this simultaneity when he said that her work 'transforms fantasy into elegance', with fantasy surely representing the avant-garde, in particular Apollinaire's own brand of Dada, and elegance representing the mainstream trend of Art Deco. Positioned at the intersection between the two, Delaunay's textiles were unprecedented.

In 1953 the Institute of Contemporary Arts in London held the exhibition *Painting into Textiles* in an effort to give a broader context to the significant sway contemporary painting was then

Lucienne Day
Herb Anthony
1950s
The Whitworth Art
Gallery, Manchester

29

enjoying over textiles. The paintings of Joan Miró (1893–1983) played a pivotal role in this dialogue, both directly, through a series of Modern Master designs commissioned by Fuller Fabrics to which he signed his name, and indirectly, by galvanising the output of designers such as Lucienne Day (b. 1917). Day took her lead from Miró's later works, a canny ploy considering how these paintings already evidenced strong decorative leanings. In fact, Miró's sense of colour did not come into its own until the 1930s, when his drawing and overall design also significantly developed. At this time, his line became bolder and simpler, its inflections easier to make out and quantify, the compositions it articulated were less agitated by small clusters of shapes and were instead organised by bolder forms. *Dancer Listening to Organ Music in a Gothic Cathedral* of 1945 is a case in point, its overall black background being centred with a grey blob, over the top of which squiggly cartoon-like characters vie for space with areas of tingling colour. Fabrics by Day such as *Herb Antony* from the mid-1950s, are perhaps the most dynamic of those derived from an interpretation of Miró because they are the most independent from their source. In *Herb Antony* the linear bird-like motifs drawn in white are boldly set-off against a pitch-black background and punctuated with yellow, green and red shapes. The anxious rhythms of Miró's paintings are repeated but its appurtenances are squeezed out until the rhythms serve purely decorative ends.

Abstract painters from the later 1950s and early 1960s such as Kelly and Richard Anuszkiewicz (b. 1930) also dabbled with textile design but not to the same extent as Delaunay and Matisse. Only Andy Warhol pursued this penchant for simultaneity with the same degree of verve in the 1960s, albeit by completely reconfiguring the relationship between painting and fabrics through his voracious appetite for glamour. Starting when he was still an illustrator in the 1930s, his quest achieved a height of sorts in 1961 with a window dressing scheme for the Bonwit Teller department store in New York, for whom he slipped a number of his hand-painted Pop works behind a series of mannequins clothed in the latest A-line dresses. A much smoother rendezvous between art and fashion occurred later in the same year when Warhol devised the fabric for a number of Stephen Brice dresses, and then even more so in 1964 when he delivered his most succinct statement yet with the *Brillo Box Dress*, a full-length number with a Brillo motif accentuating the wearer's *derrière*. In collaboration with the fashion designer Halston (1932–90), Warhol succeeded the *Brillo Box Dress* in 1972 with his flower print motif spattered across a free flowing, three-quarter length, strapless dress. The dress is classic early 1970s: the neckline plunges as low as the split of the skirt reaches high and the large candy-coloured flowers are set off against the darker green and black background, flowing perfectly with the loose fabric as it glides in tempo with the wearer to lend her an air of sultry langour – especially if she happens to be Lauren Hutton. In the mid-1970s Warhol assembled myriad fragments of designed fabrics, some by Halston, to produce a series of 'composite dresses' that pre-date the so-called 'deconstructive' designs of Rei Kawakubo (b. 1942) and Martin Margiela (b. 1959) from the 1980s. Warhol maintained a thoroughly

Andy Warhol
Brillo Box Dress
Private Collection

flexible relationship between his paintings and fashion designs, his entire oeuvre channelled through his magazine *Interview*.

The only artist to significantly extend these ideas today is Takashi Murakami. Just as Warhol drew on the imagery of his vernacular culture, so does Murakami, the difference being that Murakami's super-flat, cartoon-like figures and landscapes stem from contemporary Japanese manga comic books and animations. Murakami's paintings and their corresponding wallpaper designs – loosely based in principle on Warhol's cow wallpaper from the mid-1960s – are ultimately geared towards creating a smooth plane. The paintings are endless flat landscapes populated by Murakami's cast of characters who teem across the surface in playful abandon: odd creatures with cutesy names, mushrooms with dopey eyes and curly lashes. Despite his collaboration on a reversible raincoat with Issey Miyake (b. 1935) in the late 1990s, Murakami chose not to turn his vocabulary to the ends of dress design, and instead conspired with fashion guru Marc Jacobs (b. 1963) at Louis Vuitton in 2002 to produce a series of fabric designs. The most striking of these are being used to catapult the fashion house's accessories into the future by refashioning their hand luggage. The classic brown and tan leather of before has given way to bright pastel shades – lemon yellow, lilac and sky blue set off against either ivory white or jet black – which intertwine the LV motif with Murakami's signature winking eyes and flowers. A striking animation acts as an advertisement for the fashion house by spinning a story around one of Murakami's characters who has had her

LV bag stolen. Murakami is thus close to Warhol and Matisse in the way he rides the notion of simultaneity, opting to collaborate with others on such projects to effectively extend his ideas into new domains.

Tobias Rehberger manipulates pattern in an entirely different way. For a work entitled *Two Men's Suits (Grey/Brown)* produced in 1995, Rehberger produced two plain grey suits made of English wool and invited his gallerists at Hammelehle and Ahrends in Stuttgart, to wear them. Since they had been tailored to the artist's figure, even to a non-discerning eye it was clear that the suits did not look quite right. On one gallerist it was just the legs that were a little too long, while on the other, not only were the trousers too long, this time noticeably so, but the jacket was also far too big. Yet it was precisely in these details that the crux of the work lies: to wit, a self-portrait shrewdly displayed *on* the gallerists rather than just *by* them. A further work was initiated through an advertisement Rehberger was commissioned to design by his gallerists at Neugerriemschneider in Berlin to inform the readers of *Frieze* and *Artforum* of the gallery's 1997 exhibitions programme. The advertisement was structured around a centralised white grid motif on a black background; the grid was then broken by a series of pastel-coloured discs bouncing in and around its frame. In the same year, Rehberger followed this design through into three dimensions with an installation entitled *Brancusi*, which was based on the same elements and in which the black background and the frame of the advertisement became the walls of the gallery, while the discs popped up into seats. The finishing touch was

provided by a series of knitted jumpers based on the same configurations: *neugerriemschneider. frieze* 1997 and *neugerriemschneider. artforum* 1997. Rehberger here forged a connection between his design work for the gallery and his artwork, and then related them to a third element realised in the form of clothing. A loop was thus created that linked art and design. Rehberger has no desire to set up an atelier or factory to deal with the production of the work once it moves outside painting. Collaboration for Rehberger, as for Warhol and Murakami, implies a meeting in which everyone pools their skills.

In contrast, the second approach to design and decoration tends to forfeit the notion of simultaneity and instead foregrounds a strict theoretical or political programme. To a large extent this approach was developed by Russian Constructivist Varvara Stepanova (1894–1958) in her essay 'Present Day Dress – Production Clothing' from 1923, in which she posited a concept of dress design, the primary consideration of which was the function clothing is called upon to perform:

Fashion which psychologically reflects a way of life, customs, and aesthetic taste, gives way to clothing organized for work in different fields as defined by social movements, clothing which can prove itself only in the process of working in it, not presenting itself as having an independent value outside real life, as a special type of 'work of art' ... The whole decorative and ornamental aspect of clothing is destroyed with the slogan 'comfort and appropriateness of dress for a given productive function'.[6]

But fashion, too, has a function: to enable the individual to communicate something of their personality from

Tobias Rehberger
*neugerriemschneider.
frieze* 1997
*neugerriemschneider.
artforum* 1997
Courtesy
neugerriemschneider,
Berlin

season to season, according to their own whims. Yet despite the tone of the above quotation, there is the sense that Stepanova is far more flexible in practice than her writings suggest, and many of her designs betray a conviction in favour of aesthetic effects that are certainly superfluous to requirements. Examples can be found in the first practical realisations of her garments such as the work suit fabricated for Alexander Rodchenko (1891–1956) in 1921. Resembling a jumpsuit, the outfit accents its fastenings and storage pockets to such an extent that it transforms them into significant formal elements. While the jumpsuit is an example of Stepanova's production clothing, her sports clothing is similarly characterised by a minimal use of fabric, ease of putting on and wearing and bold colour effects. Her introduction of badges and emblems into her sportswear in order to distinguish

individual sportsmen and groups, makes the two types of clothing quite distinct.

Stepanova also turned her hand to casual clothing. The fabrics she designed for this series are thoroughly arresting as each one presses the barest of formal means – three colours and two motifs a-piece – to the most complex of visual ends. Worked out in the first instance like Delaunay's designs through gouache on paper, many of Stepanova's designs consist of multi-level colour fields in which forms gradually surge from the pattern. Executed in a limited palette, they nonetheless manage to conjure up the illusion of several spatial planes existing simultaneously. This impression of an almost structural combination of geometric patterns arises from the fact that parts of the superimposed designs are outlined but not coloured in. For Stepanova customarily left the points of intersection white or allowed the ground to show through, and thus created the optical impression of a second plane. In 1924 she initiated even more elaborate designs, enticed by the potential for creating the illusion of movement as forms transmuting into one another: of arcs becoming circles, triangles turning into rhombi. One design from this year consists of a series of pearly white and acrid blue discs floating on top of a series of red and white stripes. The different elements jar against one another so profusely that they produce surprising rhythmic effects. Their complexity means that the cut of the dress for which the fabric is intended can be quite simple without the finished garment appearing so. The contours of the fabric of the dress move with the wearer as she moves, causing the optical design to pulsate to a beat of its very own.

Varvara Stepanova
'Optical' design for fabric
1924
Rodchenko Stepanova
Archive, Moscow.
Courtesy Aleksander
Lavrenuev.
Varvara Stepanova (right)
wearing her *Optical
Dress* 1924
Photo: Alexander
Rodchenko
Courtesy Aleksander
Lavrenuev

The fabrics for many of these garments were produced at the First Textile Printing Factory in Moscow, where Stepanova acted as co-ordinator of production. As for the actual process of textile design, Stepanova felt that the artist should design the fabric from within, starting with the rules governing its weaving, so as to attain not just new decorative surfaces, but also fabrics with new physical characteristics. By positioning herself in the process of production, Stepanova could engineer these developments. It thus follows that she concured with Delaunay over the notion of the simultaneous fabric. 'We are now approaching a point when the gulf separating the fabric itself and ready-made garment,' she insisted in her 1929 article 'From Clothing Pattern to Garment', 'is becoming a serious obstacle to improving the quality of our clothing production.'[7] But Stepanova's work diverges from Delaunay's due to the fact that she did not co-ordinate the garments with stand-alone paintings and fabric designs, a practice which was the very cornerstone of her philosophy of simultaneity.

Andrea Zittel (b. 1965) is peerless among contemporary artists in that she alone endeavours to unpack the implications of some of the Constructivists' ideas for textiles and clothing. The sense of restraint so characteristic of Stepanova finds an equivalence in Zittel's output. The adherence to a strict polemic is, however, mercifully replaced with a rather eccentric spin on function, particularly on how it relates to both her own lifestyle and the lifestyle of those collecting her work. In a short article from 1994 she expanded on this: 'Working as a designer from the position of the artist is not a new strategy and was the position of groups like the Bauhaus, the Russian Constructivists and De Stijl. My departure from these movements occurs when I work with the dilemmas and the contradictions that their work unearthed.'[8] Part of Zittel's inquiry finds fruition in her *Personal Panels* 1993–8, a variety of costumes cut from a single piece of satin, silk, cotton or wool, each garment tailored to suit a particular activity, whether it is playing with the dog or cleaning the windows. When exhibited in the gallery, the costumes are placed on mannequins and presented in images on the wall in such a way that they appear to be grand monochromes. Lifted out of the gallery and put into the collector's arms, something different happens to the work. Zittel instructs the wearer to deposit their habitual clothing in storage during a six-month period so that they can truly get the most out of their *Personal Panel*. But if you are the type of person who can afford to collect this type of art, then chances are you do not need to engage in the mundane domestic chores for which they are often conceived. There is a dissonance, then, between the humble values the work embodies, and reality.

The third approach to design and decoration is to sidle up to the issue on the sly while at the same time denying any relationship with it whatsoever. The artists who have contrived this approach tend to duck beneath the conceptual cover furnished by the critics supporting them. Examples of this can be found in the writings of Clement Greenberg from the 1940s through to the 1960s, which are surely the most successful attempts to relieve the anxiety that decoration causes for abstraction.

Andrea Zittel
Orange Linen with
Red Velvet Ribbon
Personal Panel 1995–8
Sadie Coles HQ, London

Kenneth Noland
Another Line
1970
Tate

So eloquent is his discourse, in fact, that rarely does the reader question the efficacy of his persuasive argument, which may simply be about a series of stripes or chevrons. There is no place whatsoever for the notion of simultaneity in the discipline-specific story of painting that Greenberg formulates. Striving to dismiss the notion of the decorative in Matisse, in an article from 1952 Greenberg asserts that it may be an excess of the decorative that is 'responsible for the consistent failure of [Matisse's] easel pictures in the 1930s and early 1940s'. In the next sentence he then contradicts his own insight by insisting that 'far from being too decorative, these works would have actually benefited, one feels, from being more so'. [9] Thus, according to his account, it is necessary that Matisse, and by extension the writing about him, maintain the decorative in tension with something else. A work cannot be just decorative.

In the early 1960s Greenberg mobilised his not insignificant theoretical muscle in support of a new generation of artists, the so-called color-field painters. But just when it seemed as if his discourse could not get any more tendentious, the dissonance between work and text any more extreme, it did. It did when Michael Fried (b. 1939), one of Greenberg's disciples, perfected the most painstaking apology yet for the decorative:

Both [of Noland's] paintings exemplify a new level of engagement with the great 'decorative' painting of the past and perhaps with that of Matisse himself: as if in pictures like these qualities of unbrokenness, uniform intensity, and sheer breadth of color that one finds within shapes and areas in Matisse's art are recreated by – made more radically abstract – in this way, the paintings that result are profoundly anti-'decorative' in effect. [10]

The law at play here seems to laboriously decree that as the work becomes more decorative, so inversely the theory must get more rigorous. Critics contemporary with Greenberg and Fried premised numerous essays in response to their conviction for the decorative. Harold Rosenberg (1906–78) lampooned them for it: 'If the paintings' effectiveness as ornamentation were all that was in question, the determination of Noland's merits could be left to each spectator's taste in interior design.'[11] Leo Steinberg (b. 1920) bears down on the very same elements of the work but goes even further by constructing a diatribe on the back of his claim that color-field's aesthetic is alarmingly similar to the production methods associated with industrial design. So too, for him, is Greenberg's criticism, which lends sustenance to color-field painting through recourse to the writings of the philosopher Immanuel Kant (1724–1804):

This single criterion for important progressive art, moving as by predestination towards utter homogeneity of the elements of design is still with us ... in the triumph of color-field painting ... It is probably no chance coincidence that the descriptive terms which have dominated American formalist criticism ... run parallel to the contemporaneous evolution of the Detroit automobile. It's ever-increasing symbiosis of parts – the ingestion of doors, running boards, wheels, fenders, spare tires, signals etc., in a one-piece fuselage – suggests, with no need for Kant, a similar drift toward synthesizing design elements.[12]

Noland actually succeeds in maintaining both elements in play: his paintings are profoundly decorative while also being intensely felt, and there is no reason why this should be a contradiction. Of course, it is conceivable that this is

what Greenberg and Fried were actually saying, but they just felt obliged to shield the paintings from reproach. To make sense of this it is important to remember that Matisse's mellifluous shapes were contemporaneous with the distraught rhythms of Pablo Picasso (1881–1973), and that Noland's cool detachment shared the stage with the edgy vernacular of Robert Rauschenberg (b. 1925). Hence comparisons and subsequently judgements in favour of the anti-decorative impulse were inevitable. Perhaps both critics were only doing what they thought was necessary to ensure that the work received the attention it deserved.

But the story reaches its peak with Bridget Riley. While she holds Matisse in high esteem, Riley resists the decorative potential of her work, which might seem surprising given its nature. In the early 1960s she attempted this by inviting patterns to duel before the beholder's eye, resulting in a series of highly co-ordinated decorative effects that are supremely dissonant. For instance, *Fission* 1963 injects perspective, previously a device specific to figurative painting, into abstraction, and so yields a painfully warped pattern. *Shift* 1963 is premised on quite a different compositional schema: its completely regulated pattern, formed by the interlocked triangles that nudge and budge each other, occasions an overall motion. Although perspective has been eschewed in favour of flat pattern in this painting, the pattern vies with the decorative in such a way that it is supremely difficult to comprehend either. The viewer cannot quite perceive the compositional schema underpinning the painting – the very thing that would reveal what is making it jump and jiggle so. Over the next few years Riley continued to run these two compositional strategies in parallel, and then to complicate things even further, in 1964 she introduced an additional element into both, the colour grey. While in the one series the effect exaggerates perspective, in the other it works against it, leading to *Turn* 1964, which co-ordinates both strategies to the extent that tonal variance warps the flat pattern. The myriad effects produced by Riley up to this point fade, however, upon encountering the resplendent sparkles that emanate from *Arrest 2*, which marks Riley's first subtle attempts at colour prior to the full-blown embrace of 1967. Executed in 1965, it is one of the first paintings to introduce colour into the grey end of her palette while simultaneously reducing tonal contrast. Pattern delicately converges in some parts of the painting and lightly undulates in others to such delectable ends that the previously vertiginous optics are replaced by a serene mirage.

Despite these paintings being design catalysts for the mid-to-late 1960s, Riley draws her ideological line discretely before then. She is more late-1950s/early-1960s in terms of sensibility, a subtlety contemporary artists and critics revisiting the period often overlook, the result being that everyone enraptured by Riley is drawn to the reception of her work in the popular culture of the mid-to-late 1960s. Think of the fascination Jim Lambie (b. 1964) shows with her appropriation by the 1960s underground Rock circuit as being just one of many instances. So it follows that when in 1965 a dress manufacturer affiliated with The Museum of Modern Art, New York, presented Riley with a mass-produced textile version of one of her paintings,

she was mortified. The offering made it clear that the age of discretion to which she was attached was over, and that the swinging 1960s were, well, starting to swing. To make things worse, pages for *Tatler* and *Vogue* were already laid out and the mannequins in the shop windows of Madison Avenue, the very same windows in which Warhol had happily worked, were lavishly displayed in their Op art dresses. The appropriation of painting for the ends of fashion had gone much further than standing a model in front of a Jackson Pollock (1912–56) or a Piet Mondrian (1872–1944) for a fashion shoot in Cecil Beaton (1904–80) or Henri Cartier-Bresson (b. 1908) style. Not surprisingly, Riley went after retribution by enlisting the services of a lawyer – Barnett Newman's lawyer to be exact – to clean things up, insisting the art be sorted out from the design, no matter if it was 'good design'. To Riley's credit though, it was not that she could not conceive of this expanded role for her patterns, it was more the iniquitous way in which they had been copied and the inept way in which they were applied that irked her. One thing that she noted in particular was how insensitive the designers were to her compositions once they were printed on fabrics, indicating that she would perhaps have been responsive to the notion of simultaneity piloted by Delaunay.[13] Even though the meeting between art and design in Riley's work was one 1960s romance that did not take off, it is not a question of simply suggesting that Riley should have been more gregarious and embraced design, as such an approach can lead to a marked drop in standards. When Victor Vasarely (1908–97) collaborated with textile and wallpaper

Jim Lambie
(following pages)
Zobop
2002
Sadie Coles HQ,
London, and Modern
Institute, Glasgow

1 *Matisse on Art*, 2001, p.165.

2 Sonia Delauney, 'The Influence of Painting on Fashion Design' (1926), *The New Art of Color: The Writings of Robert and Sonia Delaunay*, ed. Arthur A. Cohen, London and New York 1978, p.205.

3 Ibid., p.206.

4 Colette quoted in Jaques Damase, *Sonia Delaunay: Fashion and Fabrics*, London 1991, p.115.

5 Guillaume Apollinaire quoted in *Sonia Delaunay: A Retrospective*, exh. cat., Albright-Knox Art Gallery, Buffalo, New York 1980, p.37.

6 Varvara Stepanova, 'Present Day Dress – Production Clothing' (1923), as quoted in Christina Lodder, *Russian Constructivism*, New Haven, Connecticut, and London 1983, p.148.

7 Stepanova, 'From Clothing to Pattern and Fabric' (1929), ibid., p.180.

8 Andrea Zittel, 'Andrea Zittel Responds', *Art Monthly*, no.181, February, 1994, p.22.

9 Clement Greenberg, 'Art Chronicle: 1952', *Art and Culture*, Boston 1961, p.148.

10 Michael Fried, 'Recent Work by Kenneth Noland' (1969), *Art and Objecthood*, Chicago and London 1998, p.186.

11 Harold Rosenberg, 'Kenneth Noland' (1977), *Art and Other Serious Matters*, Chicago and London, 1985, p.119.

12 Leo Steinberg, 'Other Criteria' (1972), *Other Criteria: Confrontations with Twentieth-Century Art*, New York 1972, p.79.

13 See Bridget Riley's interview with Andrew Graham-Dixon, 'A Reputation Reviewed', *Dialogues on Art*, London 1995, pp.69–70.

designers in the 1960s and 1970s, he not only produced works that were seldom engaging, but the experience in turn affected his paintings which were never again to scale their earlier heights. Contamination can thus go both ways.

Considering the present intricacies of the networks of marketing and distribution of fashion, it is no surprise that artists do not pursue Delaunay down her dazzling path by fabricating their own lines of highly patterned garments on a more substantial scale. Today it makes more sense to either turn out a few limited edition lines, *à la* Zittel and Rehberger, or else to collaborate with a fashion house as Murakami does. Likewise it is easy to see why both Noland's and Riley's paintings fostered multifarious copies in other media. Even though Noland did his stint at Black Mountain College with Josef Albers (1888–1976) and Riley hers under the influence of Paul Klee (1879–1940), and given both 'each hero' time at the Bauhaus's headquarters in Dessau, many of the school's key principles failed to percolate through to them. Had they done so, things may have been different, rendering the sneaky copies of their work spurious and the present recovery of debates around decoration and design unnecessary, as it would have been healthy to begin with. So it is not only aesthetic but also strategic ground that is to be gained by embracing design. Since specificity need not be forfeited just because an idea spans disciplines and media, a strategic simultaneity is thus a vital part of a design artist's make-up.

Anonymous
Op art dress
1960s

Furniture

2

Eighteen years ago someone asked me to design a coffee table. I thought that a work of mine which was essentially a rectangular volume with the upper surface recessed could be altered. This debased the work and produced a bad coffee table which I later threw away. The configuration and the scale of art cannot be transposed into furniture and architecture. The intent of art is different from that of the latter, which must be functional. If a chair or a building is not functional, if it appears to be only art, it is ridiculous. The art of a chair is not its resemblance to art, but is partly its reasonableness, usefulness and scale as a chair ... The art in art is partly the assertion of someone's interest regardless of other considerations. A work of art exists as itself; a chair exists as a chair itself. And the idea of a chair isn't a chair. Due to the inability of art to become furniture, I didn't try again for several years.[1]

Once more Donald Judd provides grist for the mill, on this occasion in the early 1970s when he tried his usually dextrous hand at furniture design. From his tone, you could be forgiven for thinking he was struggling with something completely new, when in actual fact he was vainly recapitulating ideas about furniture design already voiced by figures from De Stijl and the Bauhaus. So what is all the fuss about? The answer lies in the proximity between Judd's sculpture and furniture. Releasing all those glossy images of his interiors in Marfa, Texas, which revealed how he not only intermingled his art works with his design work but also with the wooden furniture of his heroes Gerrit Rietveld (1888–1964) and Alvar Aalto, did not help the situation much. Truth to tell, Judd's stack sculptures would make sublime shelving units and the floor sculptures comfortable stools.

A typical Judd plywood chair from the mid-1980s consists of a box with a back protruding from it. There are no curves, just sharp right angles everywhere. The chairs are fabricated in series, and within any one series there are variations provided by differences in configuration. Those in the side and base of the chair are a result of whether the four sides of the base are flush or inset or even absent altogether on two sides so that the light can pass right through. The only visible detailing is provided by the joints connecting the different sheets of ply from which the chairs are constituted, and even though these can be quite intricate, from a distance they are invisible and so do nothing to detract from the chairs' paired-down feel. While the chairs smooth over the hard edges of the Bauhaus with their sleek production methods, they still manage to be uncomfortable, and so ultimately are much more interesting just to look at. Jorge Pardo humorously attests to this in an interview: 'Donald Judd is an interesting artist; he's just not an interesting furniture designer. How usable is the furniture he made? You can't really sit on a Donald Judd chair.'[2] Because they are infinitely more suitable just to look at, Judd's chairs induce a sense of *déjà vu*, only natural considering that the material they are constituted from – plywood – has an extensive history in furniture design. By virtue of the fact that it goes some way in accounting for the complexity of the issues playing themselves out in Judd's work and in that of artists producing furniture today, it is important to burrow into this history, with a particular focus on its exchange with the medium of sculpture.

In the 1920s a host of designers and

Alvar Aalto
Model No.41 Paimio
chair designed for
Finmar 1931–2
Private Collection/
Bonhams, London

architects turned to bentwood and fibreboard in an attempt to produce commercially viable furniture. In 1931–2 Aalto designed an easy chair that suspends a one-piece seat within a frame. Aalto's chair is made from two continuous pieces of plywood that serve as both legs and armrests, and a further sheet that curls back on itself, creating lips at either end which neatly finish off the seat. A brace at top and bottom nimbly secures the sheet to the armrests, while a further piece of plywood reinforces the entire structure. A year later Gerrit Rietveld designed a fibreboard chair that came to be known as the Zigzag chair because the original version was formed by sheets of laminate being bent into the shape of a bolt of lightning. Then in 1935 Marcel Breuer (1902–81) created a chair for the design firm Isokon, the seat of which was cut and bent from just two

sheets of plywood. Subsequently, in 1954, Sori Yanagi (b. 1915), an assistant to Charlotte Perriand (1903–99), designed the Butterfly Stool. Also fabricated out of just two sheets of bent plywood, the stool, like Aalto's chair, is paired down to the fewest elements to gain the maximum formal effect. The two sheets of plywood are bent almost to ninety degrees so as to provide a seating area, which is finished off with a neat lip on either side. The base of the stool is formed by outwardly curved plywood, for reasons of stability, while a metal bolt joins the two sheets together. As these examples demonstrate, while simplicity is sometimes a complex thing to arrive at, there is no reason why it should be complicated all the time.

Together, Aalto, Breuer and Yanagi's plywood furniture led Charles Eames (1907–78) and Eero Saarinen (1910–61) to prototype a series of lounging chairs constructed from one shaped piece of board for MoMA's *Organic Design in Home Furnishings* exhibition in 1940, an exhibition that pre-dates the museum's *Good Design* series. The problems arising from the results led Charles and now Ray Eames (1912–88) to conduct successive experiments in bending and molding plywood by using a bizarre device they dubbed the 'Kazam! Machine' that they kept in the spare room of their apartment in Westwood, California, itself designed by Richard Neutra (1892–1970). Eames Demetrios, their grandson, remembers how the contraption was:

named not for any strange noise but for its sense of magic ... This machine allowed them to mold plywood themselves. It had a curving plaster mold with energy-guzzling electric coils running through it. Charles long remembered the terror climbing a power pole by their apartment to poach enough electricity

Charles and Ray Eames
LCW chair
1945
Eames Office

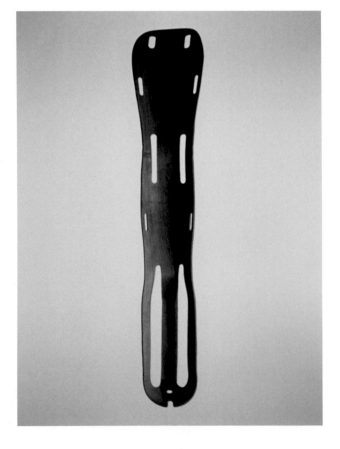

Charles and Ray Eames
Plywood splint
1940s
Eames Office

from the transformer to run the Kazam!
Machine ... They created their plywood in the
molding process by laying a sheet of the veneer
(a thin plane of wood – the 'ply' in plywood) in
the form and then putting a layer of glue on the
wood, and then repeating the process, usually
between five and eleven times. (In the organic
chair, the wood was created by laying strips
of veneer, not a whole sheet, into the desired
form.) A bicycle pump was used to inflate
a rubber balloon after the Kazam! had been
clamped tightly shut and push the wood
against the frame, giving it shape.[3]

The machine yielded both a series of
biomorphically shaped freestanding
sculptures and a commission to produce
a moulded plywood splint. Eventually the
Eameses abandoned the idea that a single-
piece shell could be viable for a chair
fabricated from wood, and instead divided
the chairs into two parts, seat and back.
The result was the *LCW* chair of 1945 and
a series of cute prototypes for children's
seating, including one in the shape of
an elephant.

Ray Eames's input was vital to all this.
Starting out in the 1930s as a painter
under the tutelage of Hans Hofmann
(1880–1966), she soon interpreted his
lessons in counterpoint as a hip
biomorphic abstraction, examples of
which abound in the documentation of
the Eameses' house. One photograph
of the interior in particular shows a series
of square canvases, consisting of yellow
and blue backgrounds with loosely
drawn circles in the foreground, gingerly
dangling from the ceiling and embodying
what Ray referred to as 'functioning
decoration'. To continue developing
her work, Ray moved to Cranbrook
where Charles was teaching in 1940.
Experimenting in various media there
led to the design of a number of magazine
covers that successfully extended the
configurations cultivated in her
paintings. One scheme for *Arts and
Architecture* boldly divided the rectangular
cover up into four unequal sections, in
each of which sat a squiggle, and, in the
top left section, a text listing the contents
of the issue. Ray also became absorbed
by sculpture, and it was an interest in
this medium, together with her creative
dialogue with Charles, that eventually
led to the moulded plywood sculptures
and the splints. Resolutely biomorphic
in shape, some of these sculptures are
relatively small and were conceived to
be placed on plinths, while others are
completely freestanding. Even though the
splints are a departure from the earlier
sculptures, by carving into them Ray
fashioned a further series of independent
sculptures. These in turn recall Aalto's
series of laminated wood experiments
from a decade earlier that he had turned
into low-relief sculptures and exhibited,
later channelling them back into his
design work in the form of architectural
detailing. Each of Ray's experiments are
key to the formal development of the
LCW chair, whose low-slung, rounded-
out seat and back rest appear to float in
space like relational abstract forms in
a painting. Thus the magazine covers, the
splints and the chair chart Ray's complete
transition from art to design while
retaining a predilection for the aesthetic
effects associated with abstract painting.
Years later, when a young woman came
bobbing up to her and asked, 'Mrs. Eames,
how did it feel to give up your painting?'
Ray guilefully replied, 'I never gave up
painting, I just changed my palette.'[4]

Richard Artschwager moved in the
opposite direction: from furniture maker
to artist. His own account of how this

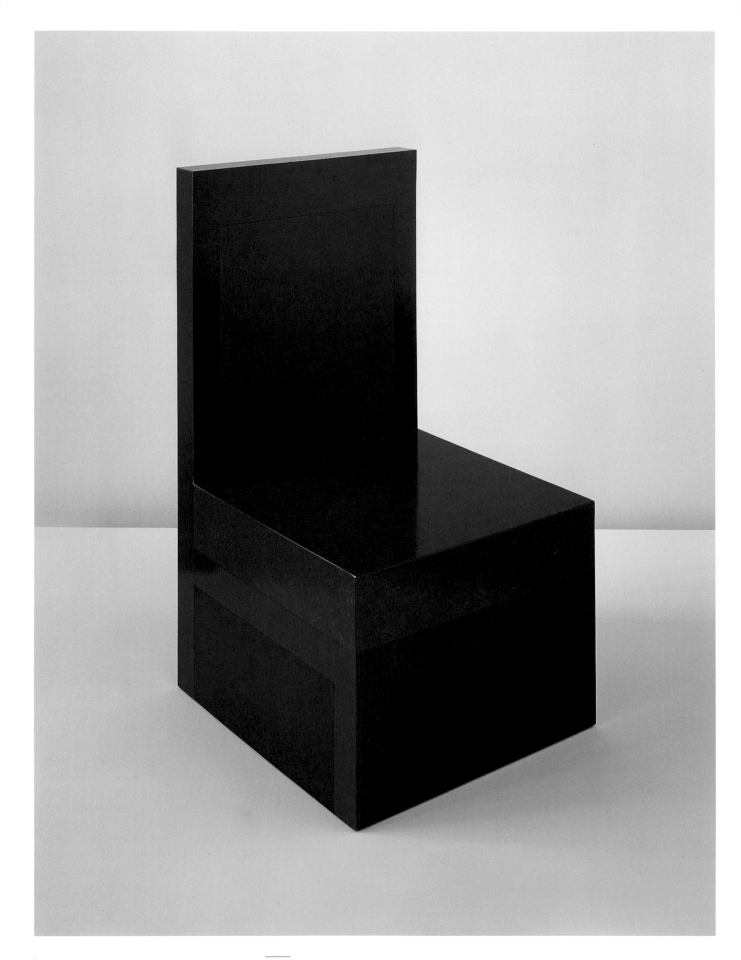

transition affected the craftsmen he employed, who were forced to shift from fabricating functional furniture to art representing furniture, is quite revealing: 'When I first started, there was adamant hostility ... With the foreman I laid it on the line. I told him, "This is not going to stop, and it's going to get worse, and you're going to live with it."'[5] In an anecdote later in the same interview, Artschwager conveys something of the tenor of the initial responses that his work garnered in the New York art world of the mid-1960s:

I had sent out about a dozen little kits – you know, with photographs and a letter – and either I got short, courteous answers, or no answer. One of the major New York museums wrote this: 'I am sorry to tell you that the Viewing Program deals only with work in the realm of sculpture and painting. After looking at the photographs you sent us, I am afraid that the committee feels that your work is more in the category of craft.'[6]

The key thing to remember about Artschwager's artwork is that it represents furniture not by means of physical resemblance, but through the presentation of an image of it. That it derives from an obtuse reading of the way in which furniture is represented in painting clarifies how it does so. Artschwager relates how the yellow mirror in *Portrait II* 1963 'could be the color of a mirror in a Fauve painting', and how in general his work is not really sculptural but 'more like a painting pushed into three dimensions'.[7] Considering that his work represents furniture, it is no surprise to find that it is fabricated using Formica, a material already representing the material it is standing in for, and one that was developed out of the extension of

a similar investigative process from which plywood was built. An early example of Artschwager's use of Formica comes with *Chair* from 1963, which is a representation of a chair, albeit a vernacular American version of a modern chair rather than the Bauhaus-type version that both Judd and the Eameses took as their point of departure. The chair's oak veneer decorously articulates the central structure, while the shiny red veneer stands in for the cushion on both its seat and back. Meanwhile, the dull black veneer filling in the sections between the legs cannily references how blank space falls into shadow and is often rendered as such by painters. Artschwager is, however, misguided to say that his work refers to Fauve painting when in actual fact it resonates more with that of Edward Hopper (1882–1967), who often depicted vernacular American interiors, such as diners and hotel rooms, littered with Formica tabletops.

As a result of the way in which Artschwager has continuously played with how Formica relates to the furniture it represents, his work became so complex that by the late 1970s and early 1980s it appeared loaded, overburdened even, with iconographic detail. Works such as *Door/Door II*, from 1984–5, are so cumbersome that they forget to do what his work does so well: to defamiliarise the most vernacular of furniture designs by drawing them through the various orders of representation that the Formica solicits. Encountering a work from this period is thus akin to having an uninvited commentator on your shoulder eagerly pointing out the fusillade of signifieds referred to in a relatively simple piece from the 1960s. A most undesirable experience. The work from the early

Richard Artschwager
Chair
1963
Kunstmuseum,
Wolfsburg

1990s such as the *Splatter Chairs*, forms a more interesting chapter in his development. This is principally because overt iconography is jettisoned in favour of an incisive commentary on his own practice to date, the humour and play in the earlier work now being taken to new heights through cartoon-like carpentry that crushes his previously overt iconography. The use of trickery in the works' play on wood and representation recalls the furniture of Eileen Gray (1878–1976), in particular a sideboard from the early 1920s, in which she amplified the wood grain to such an extent that it appears artificial, so thwarting the classic modernist notion of truth to materials prevalent at the time. By underpinning his own work with similarly nimble games, Artschwager judiciously avoids many of the pitfalls into which Judd willfully saunters. Like that of Judd, Artschwager's oeuvre is nevertheless premised on something of an antinomy. For while he creates sculpture, Artschwager also produced real furniture, hiding it from the art world until his artful representations of it brought in the money and he could desist from the production of the real thing. A contemporary artist such as Pardo instead plays across both strands in his work in a bid for a simultaneity between professional roles as well as between real and represented furniture.

Scott Burton (1939–89) attempted to blend his furniture and art into one practice. In 1980 he responded to growing interest in the sculpture/furniture dialogue by writing an article on Rietveld in which he claimed:

Rietveld is not only the first of the great 20th-century furniture designers, he is one of the great 20th-century object makers, whatever

the category of object ... His furniture-approaching-sculpture (together with Brancusi's few pieces – the *Table of Silence* [1937], the bases, the studio furniture – that is sculpture-approaching-furniture) is the major precedent for any contemporary art object seeking to extend itself toward environmental and architectural design.[8]

It is interesting how Burton articulates the interchange between sculpture and furniture through an example of an object that is in the process of transforming from one thing into another. Some of Rietveld's works are thus 'furniture-approaching-sculpture', but they never completely become sculpture in Burton's reading. Besides Rietveld's famous side table from 1923, Burton was also drawn to two other periods in Rietveld's furniture: the crate wood series from the mid-1930s and the very last furniture he designed nearly thirty years later. Of the crate furniture, Burton remarked that it 'is populist in imagery as well as in market due to its closeness in appearance to 20th-century vernacular (anonymously devised) furniture'.[9] Regarding Rietveld's late furniture Burton noted how 'to some degree you can interpret' it 'as an aged master's recalling of a favourite early triumph, the Berlin chair', since in the crate wood version 'line and plane have thickened into an almost monumental substantiality'.[10] Burton's account may be historically accurate, but it is not conceptually prudent, and so a rather literal reading of the situation results, both in his essay and in his own furniture. Because Judd's furniture is very near to Rietveld's in design and execution, his already precarious situation is worsened. While both Rietveld's and Aalto's furniture came at a time when there were few alternatives available on the market –

Richard Artschwager
Splatter Chair II
1995
Mary Boone Gallery,
New York

Donald Judd
Judd Foundation.
Office of Clarence
Judd, Architecture/
A.N. & J. Grace,
F.I. Yingling, C.,
R.C., & D.C. Judd,
Cabinetmakers.
Interior with desks and
chairs by Donald Judd
Photo: Todd Eberle

Donald Judd
101 Spring Street,
New York. Fourth floor,
dining room with
a table by Donald
Judd, chairs by
Gerrit Rietveld
and works by
Dan Flavin and
Frank Stella
Photo: Todd Eberle

Haim Steinbach
Untitled (day bed, coffin)
1989
Sonnabend Gallery,
New York

**Charlotte Perriand,
Jean Prouvé and
Sonia Delaunay**
Shelves/Room Divider
1953

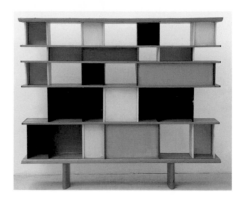

such was the motivation behind its production – Judd's arrived at the moment of the complete fetishisation of modern furniture. Judd contracted the renowned manufacturers Lehni AG of Dübendorf, Switzerland, among other companies, to construct his furniture in the early 1980s, just when modernist furniture was itself about to be treated as if it were art – something to be looked at, cooed over, paid handsomely for, but something certainly not to be sat on. Of course Judd was not to know that this transformation of the status of classic modern furniture would partly be the consequence of his activities, but the transformation was inevitable given the way modern furniture shared a set of aesthetic concerns with his art. By the 1980s the furniture-as-art market did not require more modernist-looking furniture because both cheap copies and legitimate versions – not to mention the original thing – were all available. By way of a wry comment on the situation, in 1989 artist Haim Steinbach (b. 1944) placed a piece of furniture, a day bed by Mies van der Rohe (1886–1969), in a veneered display case, evidently declaring that classic modern furniture was something to be looked at and not sat on.

Judd also fabricated shelving units, but once again they are very similar to those of Rietveld, which is unfortunate because the shelving unit has as extensive a history as the chair, with the Eameses, George Nelson, Perriand and a host of others devising efficacious takes on it. Perriand's wooden shelving unit from 1953, conceived in collaboration with Jean Prouvé (1901–84) and Sonia Delaunay, consists of five shelving sections of various widths, each of which is divided at different intervals by a series of boxes in signature Delaunay colours. While the colours lend an element of play to the terse modernity of the construction, the unit is actually inflexible in structure. Not so the Eameses' storage unit, which possesses a history almost as complex as their plywood chairs, and originates with a wooden unit Charles Eames and Saarinen prototyped in 1940 and exhibited at MoMA six years later. Only in 1950 did one of these shelving units go into mass production, although it took some time to develop a modular steel-framed version that could be tailored by the user according to their requirements. In a similar way to Perriand's, the Eameses' unit also uses colour on its individual panels to break up the homogeneity of modularity, but unlike Perriand's, their unit has chrome-plated steel uprights finished in either bright zinc or black to support the plywood shelves. Lacquered Masonite and perforated aluminium panels act as decorative shelf backs, and drawers are in plywood faced with birch or walnut. The way in which each of these elements can be adapted according to the requirements of the individual is also a crucial part of its overall aesthetic.

Joe Scanlan's *Nesting Bookcases* that run from 1989 to the present are premised on precisely how use and aesthetics dovetail in the modular work of art or design. One of the more recent samples from the series, *Product no.2* 1999, consists of an even row of shelves running the length of the exhibition space. The unit is constituted of finely crafted shelves of smooth pale wood with alternating white and lime-green accents. Twisted nylon cords connect the top tier to the bottom.

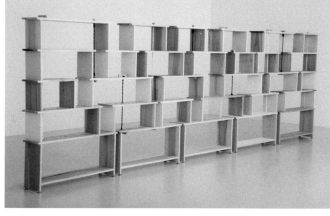

Joe Scanlan
Product no.2 1999
1999

In their essay, 'Please, Eat the Daisies', Scanlan and Jackson reproach those artists who produce art with only the semblance of use-value:

No matter how much we admire the perversion of creating useful objects whose value nonetheless stems from the pecuniary distinction of their uselessness, invoking design and function as a foil for making art betrays a troubling lack of nerve. We harbor a philosophical disappointment in the professional double standard practised by design artists themselves, whose need for art to appear useful without the risk of being so – strikes us as timid and sad.[11]

To follow through his criticism in his practice, near to the shelves in the gallery Scanlan placed a box of loose photographs, constituting the work *An Investigation on the Role of the Consumer in the Interpretation of the Work of Art* 1989–9. The images depict the bookcases in various states of domestic undress, whether they are expanded or contracted, functional as shelves and so replete with objects, or standing empty and proud like Minimalist sculptures. The images, which are actually taken by the owners of the bookcases and then mailed back to Scanlan, retroactively adjust the perception of the shelves standing in the gallery, due to the manner in which the viewer is made aware of specific contexts for what appears to be a generic object. This awareness weaves an antinomy into the very kernel of the work, because the shelving unit can no longer be seen once it is brimming with its owner's bric-a-brac. Even so, the owners complete the work rather than cancelling it out, for if the units were not used in this way by them they would surely fail to function as both art and furniture – a fiasco for Scanlan. Where Scanlan refers mostly to

furniture conceived by the designers of the 1940s and 1950s, a host of 'design artists' ranging from John Chamberlain (b. 1927) to Rehberger take the furniture of the 1960s as their point of departure. Much of the furniture of this time is referred to as 'Organic Design', a term coined by Aalto in the 1930s. Organic Design makes its way from the furniture produced as a result of Aalto's influence on Saarinen's early work with Charles Eames, through Saarinen's own series of Womb chairs and the IN-70 sofa by Isamu Noguchi (1904–88), both from 1946, and up to the seating units by Verner Panton (1926–98) from the 1960s. The high point of this trend was Panton's *Living Tower* from the late 1960s, a futuristic sculptural creation with two tongue-like seating areas offering numerous positions for one or more users. The Living Towers are fabricated in a wide selection of bright colours, from lured reds, through crush pinks, all the way to pea greens, and are covered with the most luxurious of textured fabrics. They wrap the user up and envelop them in sensuality. The eroticism inherent in this design is further enhanced by the use of Panton-derived furniture in the sci-fi film *Barbarella* (Roger Vadim, 1967). Meanwhile, the sci-fi elements are further played out by the use of the furniture of one of Panton's contemporaries, Olivier Mourgue (b. 1939), in Stanley Kubrick's film *2001: A Space Odyssey* (1968).

Rehberger revisits the aesthetics of the late 1960s not in order to subvert them, but rather to unfold the possibilities they harbour – and that includes the project to transform a Judd sculpture into a bar mentioned in the introduction. In Rehberger's work the utopianism of the 1960s is favoured over the late-1970s

Joe Scanlan
*An investigation of the
Role of the Consumer
in the Interpretation
of the Work of Art*
1999

postmodernist irony of architects such as the Coop Himmelblau group, as he strives to give the viewer a fresh phenomenological experience instead of burdening them with iconographic detail. The artist is open about this: 'After the failure of so many ideologies ... it is interesting for artists to deal with this fact of a certain claiming of absoluteness. How can we deal with this? Where does the original idea come from and how can it be used or developed?'[12] In 1996 Rehberger launched a long-term experiment entitled *Fragments of Their Pleasant Spaces*, with the aim of tracking changes in taste across art and design by basing the work on a dialogue with a group of friends who were invited to respond to a questionnaire concerning lifestyle. Rehberger fashioned a series of works out of the responses to his inquiries about their requirements for a relaxing, meditative space. The titles of these works are shaped by the nature of each individual's response: *Smoking, talking, drinking – in smoking with friends*; *Lying round lazy, not even moving for TV, sweets, coke and Vaseline*; *No need to fight about the channel, together, leaned back*. Three years later Rehberger repeated the procedure, and putting any of the two different versions back-to-back is therefore quite revealing. For instance, the first version of *Smoking, talking, drinking – in smoking with friends* is very simple, consisting of three egg-shaped stools positioned around a triangular tabletop, with a low indentation at each corner in which to comfortably nestle a glass. Although the piece is eccentric, it does not follow Panton's cartoon style, and is instead rather more akin to the futuristic 1960s designs of Kazuhide Takahama (b. 1930). The second version of *Smoking, talking, drinking – in smoking*

with friends is far more elaborate, even playful. The three seating units are fabricated from wood veneer and hug the floor, while the table is a multifarious biomorphic thing; the retro taste for 1950s sculpture and design pervades the piece, feeding on the jaunty mobiles of Alexander Calder (1898–1976) and the diffident low-reliefs of Hans Arp (1887–1996). The series will soon be completed with a third version.

When recently asked what he thought about young 'design' artists such as Rehberger and Pardo, Dan Graham (b. 1942), a key figure in the debate, made the following terse comment:

I think Pardo is looking for a fantasy of the 1960s and 1970s, but his work is luxurious in a very 1990s way. You can see that it comes from a generation that only has vague information about the recent past, which barely even knows Alvar Aalto. I always want things to be utilitarian, and I think this generation wants things to be anti-utilitarian, a little fantasy world of art.[13]

It is interesting to note how, in charging the younger generation with superficiality, Graham sounds like Judd. If Graham looked a little closer he would notice the Aalto chair discretely tucked beneath the table in Pardo's bookshop at Dia:Chelsea and furthermore how his own installation on the roof of the very same building doesn't even attempt to offer such a facility. By contrast, Graham's 'Art as Design/Design as Art' penned in 1986, and devoted to the art and design exchanges nearer to his generation, is spot-on. The essay's discussion of John Chamberlain's raw foam-rubber furniture-sculptures from the late 1960s is particularly pertinent here since Graham interprets them as a critique of the fashion for the

Verner Panton
Living Tower 1989
(designed late 1960s)
Verner Panton Design,
Switzerland

Tobias Rehberger
(above)
*Smoking, talking,
drinking – in smoking
with friends*
1999
Courtesy
neugerriemschneider,
Berlin

Tobias Rehberger
(below)
*Smoking, talking,
drinking – in smoking
with friends*
1996
Courtesy
neugerriemschneider,
Berlin

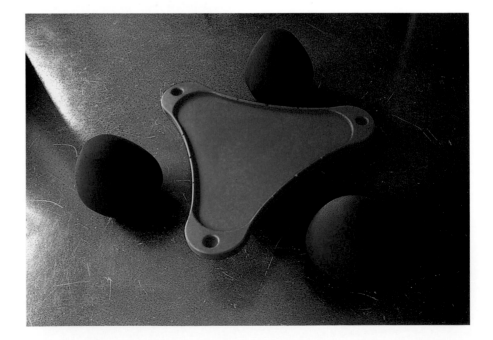

John Chamberlain
Installation view from
*John Chamberlain
Retrospective*
1971–2
Solomon R. Guggenheim
Museum, New York

Pantonesque furniture that was ubiquitous at the time:

As a conceptual comment on the design process in modern functionalist design, Chamberlain takes the logic of functional design one step further in its reduction to structural support as exposed surfaces. Rather like Dan Flavin's exposed fluorescent light tubes and fixtures, Chamberlain's couches, in their use of disintegrating foam, strip the functionalist chair of its superficial stylization to expose the material base that the functionalist chair's surface veneer covers. Thus modern design and furniture are reduced to their (industrially produced) *unseen, real* material support ... Even functionally designed chairs are designed to wear out, being part of the modern capitalist economy of built-in obsolescence.[14]

Each one of Chamberlain's sofas eventually crumbles away through use, shunning the form-follows-function rhetoric underpinning so much modernist design. Chamberlain's critique is particularly apt in relation to the furniture of the late 1960s because unlike the modernist furniture of Marcel Breuer, for example, it conceals its structure under rather portly upholstery. Graham also considers how Chamberlain's sofas impart to the viewer the opportunity to experience a very particular bodily sensation occasioned by the foam rubber, a material with structural characteristics enabling it to support the body without forfeiting its softness. As a consequence, instead of comprehending the work optically, the viewer experiences it as a tactile thing against their body; the body alters the sofa's shape as it adapts to its contours through continued use. For Graham, by placing a very large sofa on the ground-floor lobby of Guggenheim Museum during his 1971 retrospective,

Chamberlain used these very qualities as an effective way in which to react against the harsh nature of Frank Lloyd Wright's architecture. Apparently, when a visitor was actually sitting on the couch, 'its softness was experienced in terms of their own body warmth in relation to the warmth or coolness of the material and to the position and subtle movements ... of the other seated bodies on the couch'.[15] So effective was this work that Graham likens its effect to drug experiences, wherein 'the spectators experience a subjective "melting" and a floating of their bodies'.[16] The sensation of 'melting' experienced while sitting on the sofa contrasted strongly with the harsh objectivity and linear time engendered by walking up the museum's spiral ramp to view Chamberlain's career unfolding in a relatively predictable manner.

Gabriel Orozco (b. 1962) and Franz West (b. 1947) have both recently extended the implications of Chamberlain's sofas. Orozco's *Hammock at MoMA Garden* 1993 likewise criticises modernist furniture both by using an ephemeral material and by emphasising the experience of the beholder. Except that where Chamberlain was quite assertive, aggressive even, in making his point – the viewer did after all destroy the work – Orozco is more subtle. Orozco's work comprised a hammock strung up between two adjacent trees in front of the north wall of the museum's sculpture garden. As if to defy the way in which it was rendered almost invisible by the clutter of Eames chairs and tables in the foreground, the hammock strikes up a pugnacious dialogue with them in order to highlight the way in which its use significantly alters the individual's behaviour in the sculpture garden.

Furniture

Franz West
Mobilette
2000
Installation view: Franz
West, *Trog* (bottom);
Gelatin, *Untitled* (top)
Gagosian Gallery,
London

Furniture

Franz West
Couches and Seats
1989
Kunsthistorisches
Museum, Vienna

For where the Eames furniture forces the body to remain in a formal upright position, the droopy hammock beckons the same body to find a posture of repose. From this position it is not the sculpture garden that is visible, but rather the dappled light percolating through the trees. In addition, the method of fabrication of the chairs and the hammock could not be more different, and so the two types of seating are thoroughly incongruous. Orozco thus takes a stab at MoMA's fetishisation of modern furniture through exhibitions such as *Organic Design* in 1940, which not coincidentally included chairs by the Eameses.

Franz West's first furniture samples date from the mid-1980s. Welded together from a conglomerate of found metals and covered in roughly cut fabric, this amorphously-shaped furniture is nonetheless comfortable enough to be sat on. In 1989, West placed a series of sofas and divans in front of Old Master paintings in the Kunsthistorisches

Museum in Vienna. Like Orozco's hammock, they invited the beholder to rest. The sagacious placing of the furniture in front of canonical paintings, together with the way in which they encouraged the beholder to assume a horizontal position, led to an inevitable difficulty in viewing the paintings. In West's own words: 'If you look at all those things [in a museum] and you begin to feel really queasy, then you can lie down or sit down. Sitting down would be "boring", above all if it were not integrated into an artwork. So now you can integrate yourself into the art.'[17] West tends to display his furniture in series. The temporary rooftop installation at Dia:Chelsea in 1994 was a particularly exhilarating example of this development, as it consisted of three rows of sofas upholstered in brilliantly coloured and fabulously patterned fabrics which related to the various communities in the area from which they were sourced. By 1996 West was co-ordinating his furniture

1 Donald Judd, *Furniture*, Zurich 1985, n.p.
2 Jorge Pardo in an interview with Fritz Haeg, *Index*, no. 19, May, 1999, p.14.
3 Eames Demetrios, *An Eames Primer*, London 2001, p.41.
4 Ibid., p.75.
5 Richard Artschwager in an interview with Jan McDevitt, *Craft Horizons*, vol.xxv, no.5, September 1965, p.30
6 Ibid.
7 Ibid.
8 Scott Burton, 'Furniture Journal: Rietveld', *Art in America*, November 1980, p.103
9 Ibid., p.102.
10 Ibid., p.106.
11 Scanlan and Jackson, 2001, p.29.
12 Tobias Rehberger quoted in Jérôme Sans, 'Tobias Rehberger: Working With, Working Between', *Artpress*, November 2002, p.48.

13 Dan Graham, 'Mark Francis in conversation with Dan Graham', Birgit Pelzer, Mark Francis, Beatriz Colomina, *Dan Graham*, London and New York 2001, p.34.
14 Dan Graham, 'Art as Design/Design as Art', *Rock My Religion*, Cambridge, Massachusetts, and London 1993, p.215.
15 Ibid.
16 Ibid.
17 Franz West quoted in Robert Fleck, 'Sex and the Modern Sculptor', Robert Fleck, Bice Curiger, Neal Benezra, *Franz West*, London and New York 1997, p.64.
18 Scanlan and Jackson, 2001, p.27.
19 Iwona Blazwick, 'Interview with Franz West', *Possible Worlds: Sculpture from Europe*, exh. cat., Institute of Contemporary Arts/Serpentine Gallery, London 1991, n.p.

with his collages and sculptures to form fully integrated environments, resulting in a heightened emphasis on the role of the viewer.

The genealogy mapped out above reveals a tangible shift away from the anxiety that Judd betrayed apropos the practice of simultaneity. Contemporary artists turn furniture into sculpture and make furniture out of sculpture. Within this exchange, the analysis of furniture can be overtly discursive as in Scanlan's investigation into its reception and use. It can also be employed in a style-conscious manner, as Rehberger does by customising it to suit the requirements of both the individual and the reigning fashion of the day. Alternatively, furniture can be toyed with humorously, as in West's oddly-shaped and strategically-placed divans. Either way, such work presses new questions on the viewer by providing them with a new experience – for example, sitting on a divan in the middle of an exhibition – and so the work does not function merely as a detached critique. Scanlan and Jackson make a joke about just this in 'Please, Eat the Daisies':

In contrast to the institutional critiques of Michael Asher [b. 1943] and Louise Lawler [b. 1947], design art does not call attention to the place and function of art in order to question its cultural authority. Rather, it attempts to expand the accessibility of art by contriving other, more pragmatic ways of engaging with its reception and use. Where institutional critique hopes to disrupt the illusion of cultural authority by revealing the mechanisms that buttress it, design art hopes to democratise that authority by providing mood lighting and comfortable chairs.[18]

Scanlan's divisive use of humour drives home the actual comments he makes all the more effectively. The same goes for West, who neatly sums up the entire attitude, and at the same time foregrounds his own version of simultaneity in a comment on Judd: 'Don Judd said that a chair and a work of art are completely different. My understanding is that it is absolutely not different. If I make a chair, I say it's an artwork.'[19]

Interiors

3

Interiors

John Ruskin's eloquent disquisition on art's decorative function neatly dovetails with his discourse on the role of interior design. In an article devoted to ornament from 1859, Ruskin surmises that 'the only essential distinction between Decorative and other art is the being fitted for a fixed place'.[1] He clarifies this assertion in the next sentence by observing that 'the best sculpture yet produced has been the decoration of a temple front – the best painting, the decoration of a room'. Examples soon follow: 'Raphael's best doing is merely the wall-colouring of a suite of apartments in the Vatican', and 'Michelangelo's, of a ceiling in the Pope's private chapel'. And a polemical note concludes things:

[Decorative art's] nature or essence is simply its being fitted for a definite place; and, in that place, forming part of a great and harmonious whole, in companionship with other art; and so far from this being a degradation to it – so far from decorative art being inferior to other art because it is fixed to a spot – on the whole it may be considered as rather an issue of degradation that it should be portable.[2]

What Ruskin does here in a few eloquent passages is to correct the gross misconception active since the Baroque period of the early seventeenth century to the mid-eighteenth century on whose authority the portable painting came to assume its rather lofty pose at the very pinnacle of the arts. In the long run, Ruskin's thesis had a limited effect, as the dominant history of modernist painting developed by the likes of Clement Greenberg came to be based precisely on the supposition that he disputed, as did the critique of modernist painting, which continues to drowsily unfold to this day. Ruskin's discourse did, however, have a limited and indirect effect on many of the artists discussed above, particularly those fashioning entire environments in which to place their own paintings and furniture. In some cases it is as though their environments are extended out of, or are at least derived from, a co-ordination of the two disciplines, painting and sculpture, and then related to a third, architecture, without quite becoming it.

By adding a little flourish here and there, Oscar Wilde attenuates Ruskin's account of the relationship between the arts. With the moral tone of Ruskin's writing dropped, and his solemnity replaced with a florid aestheticism, Ruskin would barely recognise his principles in Wilde. In 'The House Beautiful' given as a lecture in 1882, Wilde brings his lofty aesthetics right into the reader's living room. He started his discourse by laying out the basic principles of interior design, the first of which is the importance of colour. 'A designer must imagine in colour, must think in colour, must see in colour', and 'even in imaginative art predominance must now be given to colour', since after all, 'a picture is primarily a flat surface coloured to produce a delightful effect on the beholder'.[3] Wilde insisted that colour must be applied correctly on the grounds that it resembles musical notes, for a single false one can destroy the whole effect of an interior. Rather loquaciously, he explained how one keynote colour, preferably a low tone, should be allowed to predominate, for the value of primary colours can only really be ascertained 'by having little bits of colour, beautiful embroidery, and artwork set like precious gems in the more sombre colours'.[4] Wilde found a fitting example in the Peacock Room executed between 1876 and 1877

**James Abbott
McNeill Whistler**
*Harmony in Blue
and Gold*
Peacock Room
1876–7
Freer Gallery of Art.
Smithsonian Institution,
Washington DC: Gift of
Charles Lang Freer

by James Abbott McNeill Whistler (1834–1903):

Mr. Whistler has recently done two rooms in London which are marvels of beauty. One is the famous 'Peacock Room', which I regard as the finest thing in colour and art decoration that the world has ever known since Correggio painted that wonderful room in Italy where the little children are dancing on the walls; everything is of the colours in peacock's feathers, and each part so coloured with regard to the whole that the room, when lighted up, seems like a great peacock tail spread out.[5]

Wilde noted in addition that the shutters lend the interior a further dynamic. When folded at night, the peacock's tail feathers expand like a Japanese fan, displaying the birds in full plumage, and their sweeping trains swirl in cascades of golden feathers on a glorious gold-leaf ground. Whistler's penchant for *Japonisme*, and in particular for the work of printmaker Kitagawa Utamaro (*c.* 1753–1806), is perceptible here. While the Peacock Room shares with Whistler's paintings – the Harmonies, Symphonies, and even the Nocturnes – an untrammelled delight in how visual effects in similar tones and hues seem to heighten perception, the room is nonetheless a point of departure from them. If Ruskin had seen this example of the painter's oeuvre, perhaps he would not have admonished Whistler outright as he did. Ruskin judged Whistler's painting *Nocturne in Black and Gold: The Falling Rocket c.* 1875 harshly, due to its abstract nature. Inspite of the resulting libel suite Whistler brought against Ruskin, Whistler was otherwise in agreement with the principles underlying Ruskin's writings, even if not with the precise tone of their delivery. Ruskin's diatribe against the portable picture is

indeed carefully heeded in the 'Peacock Room' and further corroborated by Whistler's own conception of the relation between portable painting and the decoration of an interior. When Whistler mocked that 'we have come to hear of ... the picture that is full of thought and of the panel that merely decorates', he was concurring with Ruskin.[6]

In spite of the squabbling between these artists and critics, they galvanised a generation of some of the most zealous designers and architects, loosely grouped under the umbrella of Art Nouveau. *Ladies Sitting Room* 1900, by Georges de Feure (1868–1928), is a consummate example of the tendency, as it fashions each and every aspect of the room in exaggerated organic forms. The room's side chair and table both stand on tall stem-like legs, tapering off at the point at which they nestle on the richly woven and densely patterned rug that takes up most of the floor. The elegance of the sofas and easy chairs scattered across the remaining space is sacrificed to the ends of comfort by rather portly upholstery. The entire scene is enclosed by a heavy wallpaper pattern which, picking up on the vegetal motifs strewn across both the rugs and the upholstery, inflates and repeats them in a mannered excess so characteristic of Art Nouveau.

At precisely the same time that this interior was designed, Adolf Loos penned his satire on Art Nouveau, 'The Poor Little Rich Man':

The home was comfortable, but it was a strain. That is why the architect supervised it during the first few weeks so that no mistake might creep in. The rich man tried hard. But it could still happen that he put a book down and absent-mindedly pushed it into a compartment intended for newspapers.

Josef Hoffmann
Stoclet House
(with view of Klimt mural)
1904–11

Or he flicked his cigar ash into the hollow in the table designed to take the candlestick. Once you held an object in your hand there was no end to guessing and looking for its proper place, and sometimes the architect had to unroll his working drawings to rediscover the place for a match-box.[7]

The use of the objects in de Feure's interior is far from apparent – the modernist form-follows-function credo is still a long way off – and so each object is subsumed into the general style of Art Nouveau. This is what goaded Loos so. What is now forgotten is how this tendency towards unification was actually quite unusual at the time, as most interiors where constituted from a mélange of styles and periods of furniture. While continuing its drive towards the aesthetic unification of a space, many of Art Nouveau's excesses where curbed by the Vienna Secessionists who succeeded it.

Stoclet House in Brussels, built by Josef Hoffmann (180–1956) between 1904 and 1911, is a fitting example of this. The architect created a sumptuous house sheathed in marble, of which the dining room, with its murals by Gustav Klimt (1862–1918), is the centrepiece. The room's walls are recessed in three stages from top to bottom: the lowest zone is formed by dark buffet cabinets, above which is a band of light marble, and recessed behind it there sits a mosaic frieze. Klimt placed the two figurative elements of the mosaic parallel to the windows. In keeping with Hoffmann's ambition to allow the maximum diversity possible without relinquishing overall unity, Klimt unified the composition of the three panels of the mural through colour. Entering from the hall, *Dancer (Expectation)* is visible first, followed by

Pair of Lovers (Fulfillment). This latter sits on the wall that accommodates the entrance door, while the former is mounted on the wall opposite it. The third, abstract, mosaic panel is situated opposite the windows that it reflects and echoes the view outside. The warm gold colour of this mosaic is so effectively set off against the cold marble that it is compelled to shimmer. Such aesthetic effects are key to the Vienna Secession. In a sense, not only does their output steer away from a mimetic relationship with nature, it also encourages variety within each unique setting, both characteristics that distance it from Art Nouveau.

More discreet, but no less effective than those by Klimt, are the murals painted by Matisse. The first is *Dance* completed in 1933, commissioned by Albert C. Barnes to occupy the arches above the doors in one of the central picture galleries of his foundation in Merion, Pensylvannia. Viewed on the page as an image out of context, the work appears to be of limited interest, but experienced in its setting something quite different happens. For *Dance* is so well tuned to the space that it strikes up a dialogue with it, something Matisse described in an interview given at the time:

My decoration should not oppress the room, but rather should give more air and space to the pictures to be seen there. The arches were four meters wide and three and a half high. I saw that the surface to be decorated was extremely low, formed like a band. Therefore all my art, all my efforts consisted in changing apparently the proportion of this band. I arrived then, through the lines, through the colors, through the energetic directions, at giving to the spectator the sensation of flight, of elevation, which makes him forget the

actual proportions, much too short to crown the three glass doors – with the idea always of creating the sky for the garden one sees through the doors.[8]

So sensitive was Matisse to the interior and the effect it had on those contemplating the paintings hung there, that he strove to make the space more suitable to the experience. Considering that he did not just produce another painting for the room, nor simply a decorative fill-in between the existing paintings, but actually fashioned a work in dialogue with both, he expanded the very concept of the decorative. The three sections of the mural are interconnected not only by the dancers, and the sweeping abstract rhythms rendered in blue, grey and pink, but also by the placement of a dancer at the points of intersection between each section. The mural provides the beholder, standing either on the balcony opposite it or at ground level, with something to look through, like a window, thus extending the effect of the large glass doors beneath each panel. In this way the mural abates the severity of the interior architecture.

The second of Matisse's murals is actually an overmantel, conceived for Nelson Rocke feller's New York town house in the late 1930s. Although only a small component of the interior, such was the overmantel's presence that it established a dialogue with the space that is even more strongly felt than that of *Dance*. As a consequence it seemed as if the interior had been entirely conceived by Matisse, or at least in collaboration with him, even though this is not the case. The overmantel occupied one end of the room alongside other artworks and discreet pieces of furniture. A portrait of a woman adorned each corner of the

Henri Matisse
(above)
Dance
1933
Barnes Foundation,
Pensylvannia

Henri Matisse
(following pages)
Rockefeller
Overmantel
Installation 1939
Rockefeller Collection

overmantel's mildly curvilinear frame. The two nestling in the higher reaches of the composition slouched on easy chairs; the woman on the bottom left was supine, as if leaning against the mantelpiece, while the last sat erect, reading a book. Each figure was attired in an elegant gown befitting contemporary high society. The logic of the overmantel resonated with the interior, which brimmed with Art Deco trappings: heavily upholstered sofas and chairs rested upon thick pile rugs and plush drapes caressed the windows. The room was a quintessential example of how Art Deco, especially in its Moderne phase, was the perfect complement to Matisse's paintings. This inference is borne out elsewhere by the many invitations the artist received throughout the 1920s and 1930s to submit designs to Parisian fashion houses known for their Art Deco leanings. In contrast, the interior architecture of the Barnes Foundation works against Matisse's aesthetic, reason enough for his mural to counteract the space rather than play along with it.

Matisse's third mural is *Leda and the Swan,* a triptych executed between 1945 and 1946 for the bedroom of a diplomat living in Paris. The central section of the mural hugs the door, while the other two sit flush with the walls on either side, the former of the two panels predominated by white and yellow and the latter mostly rendered in red. While the colour scheme makes the three panels feel as if they are discreet units, the sinuous rhythm created by the swan, which plays off the staccato patterns in the adjoining panels, works to overcome the strong vertical lines dividing the triptych. The panels are thus quite individual and yet manage to retain an element that connects them. Only the central panel contains a figure – a fitting part of the design as the panel encompasses the doorway. This mural is far more intimate – partly due to its scale – than the two earlier ones, which is also apt considering that it is for a bedroom.

A bedroom suite conceived by poet, painter, industrial designer and architect Gio Ponti (1891–1979) in the early 1950s, pits Matisse's proclivity for bold abstract shapes against Klimt's penchant for the aesthetic epiphanies inspired by gold leaf. The result is an inter-articulated interior, both luxuriant and functional at the same time. The effect is classic 1950s, as elements from abstract painting are softened in order to render them palatable to a broader market in a strategy not unlike the one used by Lucienne Day in her fabrics. If there is a weakness in Ponti's approach, however, it lies in the way in which he was willing to forfeit specificity for the sake of making the design easier to digest. For the various elements of the interior, including the fabrics and the wood panelling, are rendered in such a way that they appear to be fashioned out of the same material. While this comfortably distances Ponti from the truth-to-materials claims of many of his contemporaries, the consequence of this approach is that disparate elements coalesce to such an extreme extent that the effect is rather flat and the specificity of each object is lost. The sense of unity Ponti was striving for is instead realised more successfully in the following decade by another Italian, Ettore Sottsass (b. 1917). Sottsass fashioned a bedroom out of elements so unabashedly readymade, and therefore separate in feel, that their coalescence is precisely the point. In *Mobili Grigi* 1970, a motorbike lies at the foot of a bed – also fabricated out of metal – which has ridges on both sides, the bottom cleanly finished off, the headboard sporting two lamps which resemble those of the motorbike. The lamp motif is carried over into the edging that surrounds a mirror placed on the back wall, linking the individual units together and establishing an environment that is coherently Pop.

Fabricated during a stint in Los Angeles, *Bedroom Ensemble* 1963 by Claes Oldenburg (b. 1929), eagerly anticipates Sottsass's bedroom suite by several years, but within the context of a non-domestic space: the work was first shown at the Sidney Janis Gallery in New York. The artist describes the piece in the following terms:

The suite consisted of a bed covered by a quilted black vinyl bedspread and white vinyl sheets: a synthetic 'zebra-skin' couch with a fake leopard-skin coat placed on top of it; a bureau with a large metal 'mirror' and imitation marble lampshades. The walls are textile with black embossed patters decorated with a pseudo Jackson Pollock silkscreen 'painting'.[9]

Such is the smoky veneer covering both dressing and side tables that they look as if they had been fabricated by Artschwager, a frequent collaborator of Oldenburg's at the time. With everything covered in fake pattern, it is no surprise that the general feeling is one of modernism gone to kitsch. The vinyl for the bed sheets, the painted paper for the lampshades and the Formica for the wood all strive to look natural through the most synthetic of means. The situation is infinitely more intricate than it first appears though, as Oldenburg was not just shifting the context from home to gallery, but was actually playing on the relationship between the gallery and the home. Indeed, Oldenburg was keenly aware of how art usually ends up in the home and is selected precisely to co-ordinate with a collector's taste in interior design. *Bedroom Ensemble* even makes a sly reference to this inevitability through the inclusion of an imitation Pollock, another artist represented by Sidney Janis at the time.

Toying with the same basic elements out of which Oldenburg fashioned his *Bedroom Ensemble*, Jim Isermann (b. 1955) once again transformed the context in the early 1980s by making an art exhibition in an actual motel bedroom in California, just opposite Disneyland. In this work it was 1950s rather than 1960s kitsch that provided the point of departure, as the wall-plaques, lamps, clocks, pillows and chairs comprising *Motel Modern* 1982, exaggerated the numerous aesthetic hankerings of the mainstream at the time, especially those for curvilinear shapes brimming with candy colours. The elements that constituted the installation bounced off one another, suspending the visitor in a Disney-like world. Isermann obtained a purely ideological framework from the motel room itself, as the furniture he installed in it was not functional. More recently the artist has begun fabricating furniture elements, such as rugs that are capable of slipping between the status of an autonomous artwork and a functional object depending on their method of display. Harbouring a tricky conceptual premise, the resulting works are particularly successful. They take Isermann away from kitsch versions of mainstream modernism and nearer to Los Angeles craft-based artists from the 1950s such as Kenneth Price (b. 1935) and Peter Voulkos (1924–2002).

Claes Oldenburg
Bedroom Ensemble
1963
National Gallery of
Canada, Ottawa

The crassness of Isermann's colours – pinks and blues – is further played out by Sylvie Fleury (b. 1961) in her *Bedroom Ensemble II* from 1998, a re-modelling of Oldenburg's earlier installation, but using synthetic fur to carry the colours of the season, lipstick red and crushed purple. The entire piece exhales a sense of lascivious sensuality, and so where Oldenburg's ensemble was a joke on the kitschiness of the contemporary style, this is a lustful rendering of a boudoir. And where Oldenburg was compelled to subvert the design and fashion codes of his day, Fleury plays up to hers, including their nostalgia for the early 1960s. For Fleury, History and Hermès are both just as suitable places to go shopping for source material. On some occasions, Fleury installs *Bedroom Ensemble II* in juxtaposition with other pieces from her oeuvre. In one such instance, at the Museum für Gegenwartskunst in Zurich, she placed it opposite a wall work constituted from a series of sound bites from fashion advertisements. Sporting one liners such as 'Lush Lips: The Latest on Injections', 'Skin Crimes: 28 Ways to Prevent Them' and 'Hot Lips: Color with Bite', the wall work bluntly drew out the implications of the lavish aesthetics served up by *Bedroom Ensemble II*.

Michael Lin (b. 1964) sets what he refers to as 'day beds' in multi-coloured environments which are often situated in areas of galleries and museums where some respite from the artworks on display is welcome. An installation at the Palais de Tokyo in 2002, entitled *Palais de Tokyo*, consisted of a series of checkered pink cushions strewn across a visual carpet teeming with pink and white flowers and red and ochre leaves, all set against a lilac background. Situated between the café and the toilets, the work occupied a very particular part of the museum. The visitor who pulled up a cushion to rest or read the exhibition leaflets assumed a position that was very different to that usually assumed in the museum. But when viewed from the floor above – the point at which the work was first seen – something quite different happened. From this perspective the floor was flattened out as if into a background upon which numerous elements – people, bags and cushions – jostled for position in the foreground. Of course, this conception of the work was revised the instant the museum's stairs were descended and the visitor actually walked into the installation and pulled up a cushion on which to relax.

Artists whose work is more ideologically rhetorical have also made an important contribution to the notion of the interior. De Stijl is a key precursor here as its conceptual premise insisted that artists, architects and designers come together in the production of all-encompassing spatial spheres referred to as 'environments'. As a way of defining the group's aims, De Stijl member Vilmos Huszar (1884–1960) critically compared them to the aims of the Bauhaus. Despite the bold programme of Walter Gropius, referred to in the Introduction, in the September 1922 issue of the De Stijl journal Huszar demanded to know where in the Bauhaus 'is there any attempt to unify several disciplines?'[10] For there are, according to Huszar, only 'pictures, nothing but pictures … graphics and individual pieces of sculpture', a situation that could only be rectified by replacing Bauhaus members Johannes Itten (1888–1967), Paul Klee and Oscar

Sylvie Fleury
Bedroom Ensemble II
1998
Galerie Eva Presenhuber,
Zurich

Schlemmer (1888–1943) with other masters who 'know what the creation of a unified work of art entails'.[11]

The interior schemes developed by De Stijl's kingpin, Theo van Doesburg (1883–1931), in dialogue with various architects, are key to the group's attempts to rectify this problem. Van Doesburg inaugurated these projects by triggering a dialogue with the interior in an indirect way, using colour chiefly as a means of highlighting an existent architectural surface. *Composition IV*, conceived for the Alkmaar townhouse of artist and architect Jan Wils (1891–1972) in 1917, is an early example of this approach. It consists of a series of three stained-glass windows placed opposite a staircase designed by Wils. The two outer sections of the window are comprised of crisp black, yellow, red, blue and clear glass rectangles; these primary-colour panels flank the middle section in which the secondary colours, violet, green and orange, are to be found. In each panel van Doesburg deployed two basic patterns in inverted and mirroring configurations, working out mutations so that the composition has the appearance of a stable symmetry, although a state of absolute symmetry is denied. The effect is indeed impressive but it hardly warrants the grandiose claims he made for it:

The recapturing of the plane, through the destruction of perspective, created the need to paint the monumental on a flat plane – as in a fresco – painting in its deepest significance. Furthermore, technical solutions were found for traditional problems of stained-glass work, and this led to the evolution of stained-glass art. Thus the absolute art of painting finds its perfect expression in its colorful and formal integration in the interior.[12]

Theo van Doesburg
Composition IV
1917
Instituut Collectie
Nederland

A year later in 1918 van Doesburg designed the floors and doors for the first floor of the De Vonk house in Noordwijkerhout, creation of architect and painter J.J.P. Oud (1890–1963). The doors of the hallway are painted in grey, black and white, with each colour delineating a different structural element – either the door's central flat plane or several layers of surrounding frames. In order to render the colour scheme independent from the architecture, van Doesburg designed the tiles for the floors as well. Besides reflecting the colours included in the doors and their frames, the tiles also contain an element of ochre that accents the ochre line van Doesburg used to pick out detail on the doors. The overall sense is that the colour scheme is more modern than the interior architecture, which is full of traditional detailing.

Van Doesburg also challenged Oud's architecture, working against it with both colour and structure. Eventually this lead to a scheme for the façade of an agricultural college in Potgieterstraat, Spangen, in 1921, for which van Doesburg worked out the colour schemes on the basis of bold contrasts, with one building given over to primary colours and another secondary colours. By implementing a trick used in his paintings, van Doesburg created the impression of planes of colour moving across the surfaces and around the corners of Oud's buildings. A schematic drawing of the colour system uses line to indicate how the planes of colour are linked not simply by juxtaposition, but by a series of complex arching and diagonal configurations that do somersaults in order to join all surfaces together. The colour system thus choreographs the viewer around

the contours of the building to ensure that they experience it in its entirety.

The final stage of van Doesburg's dialogue with architecture was ushered in by his Bauhaus lecture series presented at the school in 1921, and realised in his subsequent collaboration with one of its students, the architect Cornelis van Eesteren (1897–1988). At last van Doesburg had found an architect with whom he could collaborate who would not dilute the audacity of his ideas pertaining to architecture and painting. The collaboration with van Eesteren yielded a series of proposals in the form of both models and drawings. The first of these was a colour scheme for the exterior of a university hall for the University of Amsterdam designed by van Eesteren in 1923, as well as a vast stained-glass skylight for the hall. Van Doesburg's skylight plays off planes of primary colours loosely arranged across the floor and walls of the hall in the form of large enamelled plaques, by mirroring their primary coloured geometric configurations. The materiality of these plaques declares the independence of colour from architecture, and thus reinforces the sense of coloured planes hovering in space that van Doesburg was striving for in earlier work. The feeling of colour floating and surfing on air is even more powerfully conveyed in what van Doesburg termed his counter-compositions, a series of drawings premised on axonometric projections that van Eesteren drew for two of the three model houses that they designed together. In the counter-compositions colour itself functions as an architectural material identical to the planes that it defines. More than the earlier projects, these schemes reveal how, rather than using

Theo van Doesburg
Color Construction 1923
The Museum of
Modern Art, New York.
Edgar J. Kaufmann Jr
Fund

Frederick Kiesler
Abstract Gallery 1940s
Peggy Guggenheim's
Art of this Century
installation
Solomon R. Guggenheim
Museum, New York

colour to reinforce planes perceived individually and then fused in the mind of the beholder, van Doesburg aimed to slide colour across surfaces and so compel the beholder to move in order to experience them in space. In 'Towards a Plastic Architecture' written in 1924, van Doesburg declares as much: 'The task of the modern painter is to integrate color into a harmonic whole by placing it not on a plane surface of two dimensions, but within the new realm of four-dimensional space-time.'[13]

Frederick Kiesler, an adjunct member of De Stijl, carried this co-ordination of painting, sculpture and the interior just as far, albeit by way of exhibition design. Where van Doesburg insisted that all the elements must be unified, Kiesler opted to manipulate the work of others to fabricate his total environments. The *City in Space* installation commissioned for the *Exposition Internationale des Arts Décoratifs* in Paris in 1925, is a flexible and seemingly infinite building system constituted of thin wooden beams and panels supporting models and drawings of theatre and costume designs, thus creating a sense of tension in free space. The scheme drew attention more to the milieu it presented than its own physical presence by immersing the viewer in objects and artefacts and encouraging them to be experienced in a new way. Kiesler subsequently transferred this process into the domain of fine art exhibitions with the gallery spaces he designed for Peggy Guggenheim's Art of this Century gallery in New York in the early 1940s. The design was more invasive than the 1925 installation, as the observations of one critic from the period, Clement Greenberg, revealed. 'Unframed paintings are suspended in mid-air', he

exclaimed, 'by ropes running from ceiling to floor, hung on panels at right angles to the wall, thrust out from concave walls on arms, placed on racks at knee level.'[14] Many of the ropes attached to the paintings were anchored by imposing curvilinear structures that supported them physically while also serving a visual function. These same curvilinear structures could also be sat on.

Both Kiesler's *City in Space* installation and van Doesburg's environments were precursors to *An exhibit* at the Institute for Contemporary Arts in London in 1957, an abstract work on an environmental scale conceived jointly by the artists Richard Hamilton (b.1922) and Victor Pasmore (1908–98) with the critic and curator Lawrence Alloway (b. 1926) – Hamilton and Alloway both members of the Independent Group. The installation's slender framework was fabricated out of nylon thread while the thin, multi-coloured panels conceived to counterpoint the framework were fabricated from acrylic. The panels were arranged by all three collaborators in dialogue with one another, after which Pasmore positioned cut paper shapes around the space at his discretion. While the formal principle underpinning *An exhibit* appears to have been derived from Kiesler, the conceptual one is certainly not. For unlike earlier exhibitions such as *This is Tomorrow* in 1956 at the Whitechapel Art Gallery in London, nothing was actually presented other than the structure itself. As a consequence, *An exhibit* could appear to be nearer to a work produced by De Stijl, were it not that the installation thwarted that movement's quest for utopia. *An exhibit* was a game where the final form developed only through a process

**Richard Hamilton
with Lawrence Alloway
and Victor Pasmore**
An exhibit
1957
ICA installation

of improvisation which re-commenced each time the system was set up within a new space – the configurations of which guaranteed a fresh result. In a way the principle produced environments of its own.

In the early 1960s Hélio Oiticica (1937–80) was equally absorbed in producing environments. Like the Independent Group and van Doesburg, he too was taken with the way abstract planes of colour harbour the ability to choreograph a viewer around a given space in new and surprising ways. Quite unconcerned with his relationship to the way his precedents, the Independent Group and van Doesburg, co-ordinated painting and architecture, Oiticica responded more to the history of the medium he directly came out of – painting – with a strong desire to infuse it with a striking temporal dimension. Oiticica eloquently described this in a short passage, written in the form of a diary entry, in which he coined the terms 'color-time' and 'structure-time'. The former, according to Oiticica, designates 'the transformation of structure' away from that 'old fashioned element of representation', into a situation where 'structure rotates ... in space, becoming itself also temporal', leading him to the second term, 'structure-time'.[15] The result of these speculations was a series of installations consisting of bright acrylic on wooden boards suspended in mid-air by means of string and wire. The installations were truly dialogical in nature since the visitor had to walk around them to take them in, inducing the individual planes to lilt in the air as the viewers' brushed past. Where van Doesburg and Kiesler planned their structures beforehand, and

An exhibit was an almost scientific inquiry into the nature of composition as dictated by space, Oiticica's installations were the result of a more intimate process. His dialogue with the specificity of a space – the ambience produced by its contours and lighting, the way someone would naturally circumnavigate it and so forth – found an equivalence in the viewer's experience of his work, which tended to be a more reflective one. Early examples include *Nucleus 6* from 1960–3, that incorporated mostly rectangular elements attached to thin pieces of wire allowing them to float at different degrees in relation to the viewer's body, thereby disorientating them. *Grand Nucleus*, 1960–4, consisted of two separate groupings of rectangles: depending on the original point of orientation, the first faced the viewer straight on, the second at a forty-five degree angle. The same space was thus experienced from two completely different angles and so in two distinct ways.

In the mid-1960s Daniel Buren (b. 1938) launched his *in-situ* installations, each one using fabric or paper of alternating white and coloured vertical bands 8.7 cm wide. By working in this way, Buren released himself from the traditional role of the artist who customarily produces portable artworks in a studio, which are then placed in a gallery or museum according to the whims of a curator. In his article 'The Function of the Studio' from 1971, Buren seems to be plagued by how such traditional approaches give 'rise to the ever-widening gap between the work and its place', and lead to the 'unspeakable compromise of the portable work'.[16] Buren would no doubt be alarmed by

Hélio Oiticica
Big Nucleus
1960–3
Projeto Hélio Oiticica

how closely his ideas regarding the portable artwork correspond with those of Ruskin.

Buren has divided his time since 1975 between making installations such as the one described above and another series he refers to as *Exploded Cabins*, which consist of a number of wooden structures covered in his signature stripes. The cabins are more overtly architectonic than the other installations, but they are still conceived *in situ* and so take much of their character from the space in which they are realised, setting up a tension with it through their often bizarre structural attributes. To begin with the cabins were relatively simple, but by the 1980s they had become quite elaborate, baroque even, in their construction. The installation entitled *Une Enveloppe Peut en Cacher une Autre* from 1989 is a case in point. It was so elaborate that it consisted of two parts: a shell enveloping the Centre d'Art Contemporain in Geneva and a series of cabins within the gallery. For the exterior manifestation of the work, canvas squares were wired to a grid of scaffolding and then fixed to the sides of the museum; in front of these were walls of vertically striped black and white material. These screens of fabric were cut on the diagonal from their top to bottom corner, so permitting the building to jut out from behind them. Inside the gallery, nine of the ten identically structured cabins were disseminated around the space in a symmetrical and centred fashion – two parallel columns and archways that were part of the architecture divided the space into three parts. The tenth cabin, although in line with the others, stood by itself outside the otherwise rectangular floor area. Each cabin was coloured in white stripes

Liam Gillick
Big Negotiation Screen
1998
Robert Prime, London

partnered with either black, light grey, bright green or pink stripes. The cabins appeared to burst out of the confines of their cubical format due to the fact that each square panel making up the cabin's walls had been cut on the diagonal to produce wing-like elements that projected out from the two opposite corners of the cabins. With their walls exploded, each cube acted in unison to break up the entire exhibition space into multiple vistas that invited the visitor to traverse their panoply of colours and surfaces. The work refers to painting through the wooden stretcher-like units from which each square unit is formed, to sculpture by means of the structure of the cabins themselves, and to architecture because it strikes up a dialogue with both the exterior and the interior of the building.

Buren's environments, along with those of van Doesburg and the Independent Group, are re-staged in the recent installations of Liam Gillick, but in a discreet manner so that they avoid pastiche. The paradigm of artists' environments is instead teased out further by Gillick's incorporation of textual elements that are less didactic and more narrative-driven than those used by his forebears. That said, the narratives of Gillick's books such as *The Big Conference Centre* 1997, turn on avant-garde design and its engagement with a broad spectrum of subjects. As a consequence, in a sense the multi-coloured environments Gillick presents are there to frame these elements and not literally to present them. Literally is the key word here, for when van Doesburg nurtured a fresh way to use colour to articulate a space, it allowed the viewer to traverse it in an entirely new way. Likewise,

when Buren highlights the architectural intricacies of a given place in order to uncover its inherent politics, he prompts the viewer's awareness, and so it is the interrelation between the viewer and the space that is the work. The efficacy of Gillick's position lies instead precisely in just how he re-works both approaches by 'mixing' them within ambient space.

In one such environment, *Big Negotiation Screen* 1998, Gillick stood an anodised aluminium and Plexiglas structure in front of the viewer. As the light refracts through it, orange, blue and red coloured shafts of light are projected onto the viewer. Since, in Gillick's words, the panels 'project a subtle presence that alters the colour of shadows', they operate 'quite delicately' with important 'residual effects'.[17] Thus they are in no way literal. Copies of the books or sound and video elements relating to Gillick's installations may be nearby, perhaps positioned on a shelf or simply strewn across the floor; alternatively these elements may only be present in the mind of the visitor through previous knowledge of the work.

The potentiality to correlate both painting and sculpture with architecture without actually manifesting the outcome as architecture *per se* can thus be nurtured in myriad ways. Whether or not the artist works collaboratively with an architect, as in the case of Klimt with Hoffmann, or strikes up a dialogue with an existing interior, like Matisse, the impetus towards the interior in both modern and contemporary art is irrefutable. In fashioning environments, artists such as Oldenburg and Fleury evince a desire to create their own spaces by combining elements derived from both sculpture and painting, thereby evoking the context of the gallery in

1 Ruskin, 1956, p.74.
2 Ibid.
3 Oscar Wilde, 'The House Beautiful' (1882), *The Collins Complete Works of Oscar Wilde*, London and New York 2001, p.916.
4 Ibid.
5 Ibid.
6 James Abbott McNeill Whistler, *The Gentle Art of Making Enemies* (1890), New York 1967, p.138.
7 Adolf Loos, 'The Poor Little Rich Man' (1900), *Spoken into the Void: Collected Essays 1897–1900*, London and Cambridge, Massachusetts 1982, p.126.
8 Matisse, 2001, p.110.
9 Claes Oldenburg quoted in 'Art as Design/Design as Art', Graham, 1993, p.215.
10 Vilmos Huszar quoted in Frank Whitford, *Bauhaus*, London 1984, p.116.
11 Ibid.

12 Theo van Doesburg quoted in Joop Joosten, 'Painting and Sculpture in the Context of De Stijl', *De Stijl 1917–1931: Visions of Utopia*, exh. cat., Walker Arts Center, Minneapolis 1982, p.57.
13 Ibid., pp.184–5.
14 Clement Greenberg, 'Review of the Peggy Guggenheim Collection', *The Collected Essays and Criticism*, ed. John O'Brian, vol.1, Chicago and London 1986, p.140.
15 Helio Oiticica, 'Color, Time and Structure (21 November 1960)', *Helio Oiticica*, Barcelona, 1992, p.34.
16 Daniel Buren, 'The Function of the Studio', *October: The First Decade: 1976–1986*, eds. Joan Copjec, Douglas Crimp, Rosalind Krauss, Annette Michelson, Cambridge, Massachusetts, and London 1987, p. 204.
17 Liam Gillick, 'The Semiotics of the Built World', *Liam Gillick: The Woodway*, exh. cat., Whitechapel Art Gallery, London 2002, p.82.

an ideological rather than a formal way. Meanwhile, van Doesburg and Gillick strive to create entire environments in which they oversee all variables, at times working in dialogue with architects, whether in an advisory capacity like Gillick or as an equal partner in the case of van Doesburg's collaborations with van Eesteren. Either way, the notion of simultaneity really comes into its own. The only thing these artists apparently do not do is actually produce architecture in its own right.

Architecture

4

Contemporary artists have excelled in the production of two principle kinds of architecture: the fixed and the mobile; the former is situated on a particular site, the latter is not. Within both categories there is a further division, namely, into the clean Bauhaus type, sporting crisp angles and clean materials such as glass and metal, and the unconventional R.M. Schindler (1887–1953) type, proud of its cacophony of woods and inexpensive plastics. Where the Bauhaus type was important to earlier art and architectural debates developed by the likes of Dan Graham, the Schindler type has recently been rediscovered by artists of Jorge Pardo's generation.

Graham's pavilions are a good starting point as they bundle together a host of architectural references and meld them into a tightly conceived and precisely realised set of scenarios. Each scenario is premised on an inquiry into the way in which the International Style allegedly utilised glass as a means of exposing the inner mechanics of a building to the outside in order to render relationships between interior and exterior transparent, and thus create a truly democratic form of architecture. In his essay, 'Art in Relation to Architecture/ Architecture in Relation to Art' published in 1979, Graham conjectured:

The glass gave the viewer the illusion that what was seen was seen exactly as it was. Through it one saw the technical workings of the company and the technical engineering of the building's structure. Yet the glass's literal transparency not only falsely objectified reality, it was a paradoxical camouflage. For while the actual function of the occupying corporation might have been to concentrate its self-contained power and to control by secreting information, its architectural façade gave the impression of absolute openness.[1]

Of particular interest to Graham was how, once exiled from their base at the Bauhaus in Germany to America, exponents of the International Style such as Mies van der Rohe (1886–1969) subverted their initial reasons for deploying the material by using reflective glass. The use of reflective glass appears all the more deceptive since it lends the illusion of transparency to a material that can behave more like a mirror, reflecting the public space back onto itself while maintaining the privacy of the interior. Sleek empires of steel and glass such as Mies van der Rohe's Seagram Mural Building from 1954–8, use a kind of gold or bronze tint to render the effect all the more disorientating to the passer-by.

In response to the prevalence of such buildings in many cities, Graham constructed the first of his pavilions, *Public Space/Two Audiences*, in 1976. A sheet of sound-insulating glass and a sheet of two-way mirrored glass divided the space. For the viewer, the glass dividers represented a visual window showing and objectifying the behaviour of other visitors visible on the other side of the glass walls. The visitors, who could be observed but not heard, became by analogy a 'mirror' of the outward behaviour of the original viewer. At the same time, the two-way mirror allowed those in the space to in turn observe themselves as a unified body engaged in looking at others. The complexity of the relationship of the viewers to their own image, as well as to the image of the other visitors, was echoed in a second reflection, in addition to that of the mirror, coming from the glass. In the terms of Graham's inquiry, the

Mies van der Rohe
Seagram Building,
New York
1954–8

effect was to render visible the social and psychological effects of the pavilion, its use of glass in particular.

Graham soon began to situate these experiments in everyday circumstances, one such example being *Clinic for a Suburban Site* from 1978. The proposal consists of a two-level structure on a hill; only the top pavilion-like structure is visible from the street. The clinic is made up of a waiting room with a front façade of a single plane of transparent glass and a consultation room, the division between the two being articulated by a glass sliding door. At the far end of the consultation room is a mirror, reflecting the activities of both of the rooms and of the outside. According to Graham, 'in *Clinic for a Suburban Site*, the placement of the mirror gives observers, in either of the two inner rooms or outside the building, a view of the position of their gaze and of the gaze of others'.[2] Moreover, by way of articulating a response to the International Style's use of glass, the work 'shows the social, frontal spaces separated from each other and from Nature'.[3]

In the same year Graham extended the investigation into glass in a suburban setting in *Alteration to a Suburban House*. The model shows a classic ranch-style suburban house; its façade has been cut away and replaced with a single large sheet of transparent glass. Halfway into the house and cutting it in half lengthwise, Graham placed a large mirror, the same width as the sheet of glass to which it sits parallel. The effect is to render the interior of the front room of the house, replete with TV and dining area, visible from the street; in addition the street is reflected into the house in the mirror. Not only is the private made public, but the public is also reflected in

the once private quarters of the house through the mirror. These once separated spaces now commingle as the image of both the inhabitants and the passers-by are reflected on the same plane. But since all of this is manifested in a model inhabited by little plastic people, some strange things happen, especially when Graham gives the roles of homeowner and passers-by to figures from *Star Wars* (George Lucas, 1977), the blockbuster film contemporary with *Alteration to a Suburban House*. Never has the correspondence between high theory and pop culture been more fruitful as when the reflected images of Han Solo and Princess Leya mix in the mirror to illustrate Graham's critique of Mies van der Rohe.

In *Alteration of a Suburban House* Graham refers more to Mies van der Rohe's private dwellings such as Farnsworth House (1946–51, Plano, Illinois), than to urban skyscrapers. Thus the sheet of glass that replaces the façade in Graham's model can be read as being lifted from the façade of Mies van der Rohe's building. The dialogue with Mies van der Rohe is heightened by the fact that he tended to withdraw his private houses into secluded parks to ensure the owner's privacy, a necessary prerequisite because they were made almost entirely from glass. In this way the rhetoric of transparency is once again thwarted by the architect as a new barrier between private and public space is erected, in this instance at the perimeter of the park. Beyond Mies van der Rohe, *Alteration to a Suburban House* also alludes to the then-contemporary projects of Robert Venturi (b. 1925) that tended to reflect the surrounding vernacular architecture and so enter into dialogue

Mies van der Rohe
Farnsworth House
1946–51

with it rather than stand aloof from it.

Graham's models and their accompanying contexts are about as innovative as Graham gets, and his subsequent work is just glass, glass and more glass with the result that what was once a critique of Mies van der Rohe becomes more of a paean to him. There are a few exceptions. Interestingly, these usually occur when Graham presses the pavilions to utilitarian ends – as swimming pools, skateboard arenas or bridges. One of the most successful examples of this is Café Bravo from 1998, a structure positioned between two buildings on a street in Berlin and fabricated from various types of two-way and reflective glass. A cappuccino is usually a cappuccino but not so in this café as Graham has transformed the most quotidian of experiences into a truly vertiginous delight by presenting everyone with a panoply of images of others engaged in the same activity.

Quite a different end point is reached if R.M. Schindler's architecture is taken as the point of departure for contemporary practice. Initially assumed to be a member of the International Style – although surely rather an idiosyncratic one as he dressed in open-collared silk shirts and sandals rather than the ubiquitous bespoke suits and brogues of the profession – Schindler was soon sidelined in his adopted home city of Los Angeles. The consequence was a positive one: never has a modern architect been so sensitive to the particularities of a region and certain localities within it. That Schindler shunned the very notion of a generic style as adopted by his more popular contemporaries of the International Style in favour of a philosophy that fabricates specific spaces in response to particular places, was an indication of the extent to which his work would be largely misunderstood in his own lifetime. So too did the occasional swipes he took at the International Style, like this one from his article 'Space Architecture' penned in 1934:

The classical code of set forms for columns, architraves, and cornices, is replaced by stereotyped vocabulary of steel columns, horizontal parapets, and corner windows, all to be used equally, both in the jungles and on the glaciers.[4]

Schindler's wit is evident here especially as numerous exponents of the style simply produced the same building again and again with little sensitivity to the site. Mies van de Rohe deployed the same basic scheme repeatedly in his buildings, no matter the city or the use they were intended for. Therefore it is as autonomous objects that his work is enjoyed. So it is fitting that in a further essay from a decade later Schindler composed a critique specifically aimed at Miesian glass architecture. The essay asserts that architecture will reach its apotheosis only when the architect has mastered the use of light, 'and his power will be complete when the present primitive glass wall develops into the translucent light screen'.[5] Light was so important to Schindler that merely flooding a space with it was not enough. For the architect who referred to his entire output as 'space architecture', it was precise articulation that counted.

Schindler derived many of the formal characteristics of his buildings from their sites, which varied considerably according to the particularities of both

Dan Graham
Café Bravo
1998
Marian Goodman
Gallery, New York

R.M. Schindler
(previous pages)
Tischler House,
(interior view)
1950

R.M. Schindler
(below)
Tischler House
(exterior view)
1950

the plot the clients had bought and their often unusual ideas for inhabiting them. Naturally there were certain basic tenets to which he adhered, such as the use of the L-Shaped plan, but these were expanded and developed according to need. Tischler House in Westwook, California, from 1950, is a case in point. The house is spread over three levels, much of the top one being taken up by a central living room that converges around an eating nook enclosed by a brick fireplace. Everything about the room is unusual. From the traditionally shaped roof and its panels of blue corrugated fibreglass, to the large sheet of aluminium surrounding the fire place, each detail brings with it a type of eccentricity. This is Schindler-style ornament.

Such attributes contrast Schindler sharply not only with Mies van der Rohe, but also with Richard Neutra, an architect with whom he worked for a time. Nowhere is this more evident than when comparing Tischler House with Neutra's Kaufman House in Palm Springs from 1946. The round steel columns that Neutra introduced to support elements of the structure are rather poised, almost slender, and the house's glass walls are refined to the point of physical fragility. An outdoor area that is semi-enclosed separates these sections of the house from the guest wing, and the undulating desert landscape that forms a suitable backdrop to both is spotted with boulders that act like bushes. The effect is very similar to Mies van der Rohe's glass houses from the same period: the house is clean-cut and situated in a luscious flat landscape from which it stands proud. These principles were used even more persuasively in the Case Study Program, a sort of regional flowering of the International Style

for which Neutra, along with a host of other architects including the Eameses, designed houses. The programme, the result of a competition launched in 1945, was intended to give a select group of modern architects the opportunity to indulge in their wildest fantasies and in some cases, live in them. The idea was that it would be gratifying for the architects to bask in the glory of their accomplishments from the comfort of a Marcel Breuer chair overlooking the serene Californian landscape. They all did, too, except Schindler, who was not invited to participate.

The Los Angeles Museum of Contemporary Art (LA MOCA) re-staged aspects of the Case Study Program in an exhibition in 1989. The fake lighting and painted scenery that stood in for a once-lush reality made the houses feel like part of a theatre set; fitting, given the way in which the architecture established such a staged dynamic with both the landscape and its inhabitants, especially as captured in the lustrous photographs of Julius Shulman (b. 1910). Numerous art students enthusiastically visited the exhibition and fashioned various responses to it over the next decade. Perhaps the first was Sam Durant (b. 1961):

[The LA MOCA show] happened around a time when a lot of people, myself included, were becoming interested in mid-century design and architecture. It not only spurned my interest in the design, but also in its philosophical underpinnings and the attendant economic, social, and political factors. At the time of the show there wasn't the fetishization of mid-century architecture that we have now. Many of the people who lived in the Case Study Houses didn't think of them as important architecture; they were

Richard Neutra
(following pages)
Kaufman House
1946
Photo: Julius Shulman

just houses. The owners remodeled with no thought of architectural integrity: they added curtains, laid carpets, tore out kitchens.[6]

In 1995 Durant came up with a series of models and collages that respond to the Case Study Houses. *Abandoned House no. 3* shows a classic Case Study House, victim of a gruesome fire – the glass is smashed, the walls charred and much of the detailing has been burnt to a crisp. *Abandoned House no. 4* has suffered an even worse fate, with slices of its roof missing and its walls completely desecrated. In Durant's terms, the models are 'poorly built, vandalized', and are meant 'as an allegory for the damage done to architecture simply by occupying it'.[7] His montages are just as unseemly. They are made using photocopies of Shulman's photographs, and reflect the artist's umbrage at the photographer's populating of the Case Study Houses with stereotypically clean, waspish types for

the purpose of his glossy lifestyle images. In *Known Associate*, a bloated Hells Angel trundles out of the front door of a grainy image of one of the houses making an obscene sign. Another image shows a similar character relaxing on a chair and sucking on a bong. Of these works, Durant has said: 'The collages became a way to manifest an absurd and nasty critique of the more strident aspects of mid-century design. I saw the pasting in of white-trash partiers and decorative furniture as the return of the repressed.'[8] Entropy takes over entirely and the modernist dream becomes a nightmare as the Case Study Houses are subjected to incessant partying, vandalism and fire.

Pardo's response to the Case Study Houses is far more tempered. In 1994 he designed a foldout book of plans for buildings in response to suggestions provided by ten people usually involved in the production of artists books – ranging from graphic designers and printers through to binders all the way to the gallerists distributing the books. The appropriately titled *Ten People Ten Books*, contains architectural plans that the owner of the book may choose to realise if they wish. Four years later, Pardo realised one such plan with a little help from LA MOCA who commissioned *4166 Sea View Lane* as part of their exhibition programme. Once the house was finished and closed to visitors, the artist moved in.

4166 Sea View Lane is situated in Mount Washington, Los Angeles, on a sloping hillside. While at first Pardo kept the garden carefully, now vegetation runs wild and camouflages much of the windowless exterior walls of the house. Only when turning into the U-shape of the courtyard does something of the house's interior begin to reveal itself,

Sam Durant
Abandoned House no. 2
1995
Blum & Poe,
Los Angeles

Sam Durant
Known Associate
1995
Blum & Poe,
Los Angeles

Jorge Pardo
4166 Sea View Lane
1998
Project for the Museum
of Contemporary Art,
Los Angeles

Jorge Pardo
4166 Sea View Lane
1998
Project for the Museum
of Contemporary Art,
Los Angeles

Sea View Lane, but now just reads 'do a view' or something like that.[9]

as everything, including the bathroom and the bedroom, is sheathed in glass. In one direction lies the artist's studio, embedded at the bottom of the site looking up to the courtyard and house. In the other direction is the entrance. Once inside, a corridor choreographs the visitor around a series of rooms that reveal themselves like so many events, from the bathroom to the bedroom to the kitchen and then eventually out into two substantial living areas. From here the visitor gets to drink in the hazy sprawl of both the city and the undulating landscape stretching out behind it through one of the large windows. The guesthouse is the final section to be experienced, and from its cramped bathroom a slender window looks back onto the courtyard, while a door opens onto an outdoor staircase that leads back onto the street.

An effective description of the atmosphere pervading the house is offered by a friend of Pardo's, the artist Frances Stark (b. 1967), who in the following little vignette writes beautifully in time with it:

I entered *4166 Sea View Lane*, the latest sculpture/residence of Jorge Pardo, through the studio door. The studio is office-like but dusty and, surprisingly, it's cramped with large canvases, paintings in progress. It also has a balcony. I went out onto it to wait for Jorge to get off the telephone. It was a beautiful day up there at Sea View Lane, although I could not exactly see all the way to the sea. I left the studio through a different door leading straight to a stairway and bookshelves which run along the staircase of what seems like a front entrance. I am calling it the front entrance because there is some vinyl lettering on the glass to the right of the door which used to announce, for the MOCA exhibit, *Jorge Pardo 4166*

The relaxed and informal attitude the house induces in its visitors, coupled with its clumsiness, starkly contrasts it with Neutra's designs. These qualities are nowhere more prevalent than in the house's relationship to the site, as well as in its internal layout. Neutra's Kaufman House in Palm Springs frames the landscape and is set distinctly apart from it, an effect created by its windows which are fabricated from crisp panes of glass, all tightly clamped in angular steel frames. *4166 Sea View Lane* recoils from simply framing the scenic, and instead strikes up a rapport with the landscape based on the way it hugs the hillside into which it almost blends, by encouraging the wood to weather and cheering the shrubbery on as it thickens. Not that the house is a prime example of the much-venerated notion of 'critical regionalism': its awkwardness – the lack of windows and irregular articulation of space – sees to that. The type of photographs both Neutra and Pardo commissioned to represent their architecture highlights the contrast between them even more. Once the cursory shots of Pardo's house had been taken for the museum's use, the interior shots he solicited often show the house in use as a live-in-work-in place. It is never quite clear what each room was intended to be used for since the revolving décor of paintings and rugs is as extensive as the production line of furniture passing through both its domestic and professional doors. Shulman's images of Neutra's apartments could not be more different: they freeze the interior to such a point that it seems almost lifeless. The grain of living is

Jorge Pardo
4166 Sea View Lane
1998
Project for the Museum
of Contemporary Art,
Los Angeles

R.M. Schindler
King's Road House
1922
Photo: Julius Shulman

lost to the gloss of the image.

The playful use of materials, the unusual articulation of space and the eccentric use of colour all forge points of correspondence between Schindler and Pardo. Rather than the Tischler House, comparing *4166 Sea View Lane* with the Kings Road House from 1922, in West Hollywood, is more conducive to sparking a dialogue. Of this building the architectural critic and one-time member of the Independent Group, Reyner Banham (1922–88), observed that:

much of the construction is in wood and quite light – the roofs, the glazed sleeping porches on the roofs, and the sliding glazed walls that look into the system of half-enclosed courtyards that are what the design is really all about. The construction techniques are clever throughout but also have a highly improvised air. The whole thing has the freshness of a brilliant and highly trained European talent learning to relax and enjoy himself in a California whose golden legend has not yet been smirched by smog.[10]

Also built for his family and as a live-in-work-in space, the Kings Road House is one of Schindler's most challenging buildings because it introduces new ways of living in a house. Although the house was set up to grant two couples intimacy from one another by introducing separate living rooms and bathrooms, large communal living areas actually run in between these spaces, sleeping baskets substitute for bedrooms, and Schindler also set up his office at the same location. Quite different in both configuration and its means of fabrication to *4166 Sea View Lane*, it was nevertheless built for a similar purpose with the same degree of sensitivity to location.

Besotted commentators who are only too delighted to wax on about the way in which Pardo 'blurs boundaries' and 'tests disciplines' often overlook the specificity of his gestures. Collaboration, both with a client and other professionals, which is a key aspect of the design and architectural process, scrambles traditional notions of artistic authorship, but ultimately Pardo is not willing to dissolve his voice in the team effort that goes with the territory. 'I'm interested in utilising the design team rather than working with the design team to be honest, because I see this as a work that I'm making and I don't see it as a social, collaborative thing – which is different.'[11] Pardo perceives himself in quite conventional terms as an artist and so it is no surprise that in a different interview he also states: 'I don't feel comfortable as an architect and I don't feel comfortable as a designer, because I'm not [either].'[12] These plain declarations find their counterpart in the unusual qualities of his house, both from the outside, due to the lack of windows, and on the inside, due to the shoddiness of some of the fittings. Clearly, there is an element of explorative amateurism about the house that must be significant as Pardo could quite easily have contracted out the blueprints or just imported a pre-fabricated house as a ready-made. Since he does neither, it follows that it is the traditional creative role of the artist that interests him, albeit a role threaded through the myriad loops of a simultaneous practice as he nimbly turns his hand to fashioning works out of different media and their associated disciplines. But there is the distinct sense coming from all of this that Pardo is having his cake and eating it: for he has made a suave avant-garde gesture by rendering a sculpture as a house and at the same time has created something eye-

catching. While in one sense the work is challenging, a true commingling of art and life, in another sense it is the cherry on top of the icing on top of the cake, as Pardo now has a stunning house to live in, partly paid for by a museum.

Pardo's gesture is better grasped when it is set next to one of the few buildings designed by a modern artist, Matisse's Chapel of the Rosary, completed in 1951. Matisse directed every aspect of this building: from its exterior shape right the way through to its liturgical vestments. The chapel is based on a thick L-shape, with the altar at the bend, the nave in the long arm and the nuns' transept in the shorter. Splayed across one wall of the nave is a ceramic mural, *Virgin and Child*, while the *Stations of the Cross* occupies the wall opposite the altar, behind which there is a third mural, *St. Dominic*. Illuminating the murals and the room in general are the stained glass windows that together constitute *The Tree of Life*, six elements of which sit opposite *Virgin and Child* and two behind the altar. While Matisse and Pardo evidently share an unfettered delight in design and ornament, they derive their language from very different bases. The Chapel of the Rosary accrues its spatial characteristics from painting and drawing, whereas *4166 Sea View Lane* clings to the possibilities offered by sculptural form. While Matisse's chapel contains numerous sculptural elements such as the crucifix, and Pardo's house features painterly elements, the opposing sensibilities are palpable in each of their buildings. In the final analysis, Pardo's is the more successful because his sensibility is far closer to architecture. Perhaps Matisse could not devise a new technique akin to the cut-outs to deal with the actual concrete building and its detailing; as a result his design is a somewhat humdrum box in which his scintillating murals and sparkling windows are placed. It is true that Matisse has the more difficult job, the widest gap to breach, but through his recourse to Schindler's 'Spatial Architecture' Pardo manages to pull off the more considerable feat.

In their book *Ordinariness and Light* published in 1970, the one-time members of the Independent Group Alison and Peter Smithson surmised that:

For some people the caravan provides a 'home' – with little or no outlay on furnishings – which is technological, twentieth century. Or there are the people who naturally, together with a few hens, in any place, form Schacksville. In the caravan you see people as they might wish or dare to be; for the caravan is the nearest thing to an 'Appliance House' that the market has to offer.[13]

Mobile houses designed by Eileen Gray and Charlotte Perriand in the 1930s make evident how architects had been applying themselves to the issues pertaining to mobile living for some time. Gray's Ellipse House of 1936 is a prefabricated unit of interlocking concrete panels that can be erected swiftly on point foundations, and its modular components, each one elliptical in cross section, can be assembled in various combinations. Gray also appended a porch and entry component and devised modular plumbing, kitchen and storage equipment to afford a degree of flexibility in the internal configuration of the space. Perriand's attempt at a low cost portable housing unit from a year later was light enough to be carried on the back and so was fully adaptable. Perriand and a collaborating engineer fashioned the

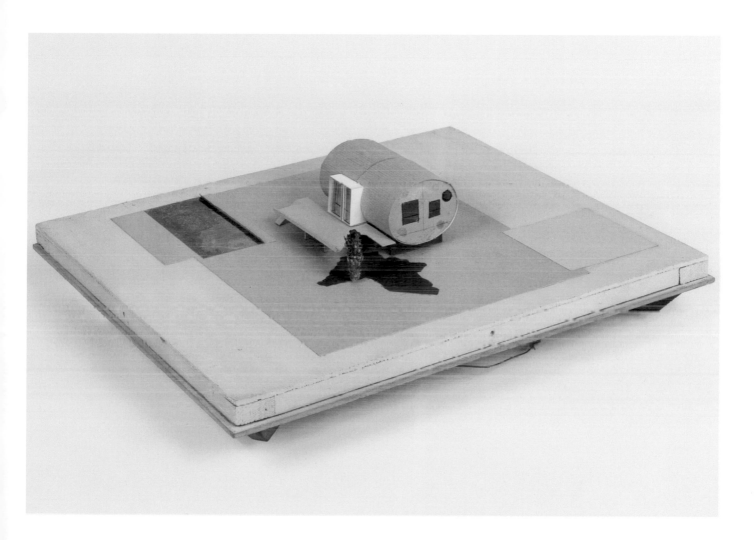

Eileen Gray
Design for a *Prefabricated
House of Elliptical Section*
1937
Royal Institute of British
Architects, London

Andrea Zittel
A–Z Travel Trailers
1995
Installation view, San
Francisco MOMA, 1996

structure from a tubular steel frame with insulated wall panels surfaced in aluminium, and they furnished it with folding bunk beds, a table and stools that doubled as storage compartments.

Contemporary artists have interpreted the possibilities of mobile housing in two ways, both of which relate to the Smithsons' quote above. The first type represented by Andrea Zittel and Kathrin Böhm (b. 1969), go for the 'Appliance House', something closer to what Gray and Perriand had in mind; the second type, spearheaded by Dutch design group Atelier Van Lieshout (founded in 1995 by Joep van Lieshout), go for the 'Schacksville' aesthetic.

Working on the same basic principle as her *Personal Panels*, Zittel's *A-Z Travel Trailers* begun in 1995 are compact metallic trailers on wheels that can be hooked up to a car and whisked away. For an exhibition of Zittel's work at San Francisco Museum of Modern Art in 1995, three teams started out from San Diego and travelled all the way to the museum in San Francisco by different routes. Each team customised its trailer and added to it *en route* according to need. Where one team, consisting of Zittel's parents, retraced their honeymoon drive up Highway 1 along the coastline of California, Zittel and her partner went via the Biosphere in Arizona, adding a lounge bed cushioned with salmon pink upholstery to their trailer. The exteriors of each unit are the same: smooth silver and institutional-green siding with a teak trim. Prior to being exhibited in the museum, the trailers spent the night in the San Francisco RV park, the first and probably the last time it had anything in common with the art museum only a few blocks away.

Böhm's *Mobile Porch*, conceived in collaboration with the engineer Andreas Lang (b. 1968) and artist Stefan Saffer (b. 1968) in 2000, is a mobile mini-architecture designed to perambulate across the public sphere and to engage on a one-to-one level with the users it comes across. The observations and experiences collected during on site residencies are a valuable source of information for Böhm not only in terms of the state and the potential of everyday situations but also for strategies that can affect the future placing of the work. The porch is a bold cylindrical structure that has been appropriated for extremely diverse ends and wheeled around numerous locations, from markets to corporate plazas. The structure opens out to reveal a sturdy platform that on different occasions has been used to read poetry, sell merchandise, watch TV and to eat lunch on. Even though its engineering gives it a clean sense of definition, over the years its use has covered it with the patina of time – not in a romantic worn down sense but in a rougher more tactile way. The result is a sort of palimpsest of use-value, which is further tracked through a series of videos documenting the porch *in situ*.

The 'Schacksville' aesthetic that Böhm's porch almost falls into is adopted by Atelier Van Lieshout from the very outset. Their mobile buildings focus almost exclusively on the client they are intended for, offering optimum comfort both in terms of their design and atmosphere. They are often dominated by a surfeit of deep-pile carpets, soft cushions, luxurious materials and intense colours, together evoking a heightened sense of atmosphere. *Modular House Mobile* realised in 1995 is a designer's take on the classic camper van. The bright

1 Graham, 'Art in Relation to Architecture/ Architecture in Relation to Art', Graham, 1993, pp.226–7.
2 Graham, 'Clinic for a Suburban Site', *Dan Graham: Buildings and Signs*, exh. cat., Museum of Modern Art, Oxford 1981, p.33.
3 Ibid.
4 R.M. Schindler, 'Space Architecture' (1934), Judith Sheine, *R.M. Schindler*, London and New York 2001, p.74.
5 R.M. Schindler, 'Notes· Modern Architecture' (1944), ibid., p.89.
6 Sam Durant, 'In Interview with Rita Kersting', *Sam Durant*, exh. cat., Museum of Contemporary Art, Los Angeles 2002, p.57.

7 Ibid.
8 Ibid.
9 Frances Stark, *The Architect and the Housewife*, London 1999, p.28.
10 Reyner Banham, *Guide to Modern Architecture*, London 1962, p.138.
11 Interview with Jorge Pardo, exh. handout, Centre for Contemporary Arts, Glasgow 2000, n.p.
12 Fritz Haeg, 'An Interview with Jorge Pardo', *Commerce*, Special Issue on *4166 Sea View Lane*, Summer 2003, p.59.
13 Alison and Peter Smithson, *Ordinariness and Light· Urban Theories 1952–1960 and Their Application in a Building Project 1963–1970*, London 1970, p.115.

yellow and orange of the live-in unit clashes harshly with the battleship grey of the truck into which it has been hauled. Inside, the section above the driver's cabin holds a double bed, while the central section is given over to the living area, punctuated by a table and bench. One of the mobile units, also from 1995, *Bais-o-Drôme* – its title adopted from the French designation of a place where the activity engaged in is sex – presents a bachelor pad Van Lieshout style, their sensibility serving the contemporary vogue for design-conscious bachelor pads. The overall feel of the other units, which display a strongly surreal type of macho architecture, is taken to its logical conclusion. On entering the unit, the 'play area' is the first section the visitor comes across, replete with mattress and blue cushions, spirit bottles attached to the walls for easy access and ambient lighting overhead. This area gives way to a central section filled with a sheepskin-covered table; the bedroom itself lies at the far end of the unit.

The move in contemporary practice towards fabricating actual architectural units thus splits into a number of sensibilities that both diverge and overlap. There are, however, some distinct traits. It is only recently that Graham has been impelled to design functional slices of architecture rather than just presenting theoretical scenarios. The benefit of doing so is that the critical programme in which he has a vested interest is almost built into the structure, which has enormous consequences on the viewer's experience as they can receive the ideas through bodily experience rather than just textual discourse. As a first-generation conceptual artist like Buren, Graham

started out with a raw critical agenda which over time has been refined, to the point at which today it is manifested through a series of slick, fabricated objects, the inherent contradictions to such a process of recuperation becoming all the more glaring as he continues. Atelier Van Lieshout only seem to recapitulate conceptual artist's critical posturing. Pardo, Zittel and Böhm have a very different point of departure, one that permits them to maintain once seemingly contradictory tendencies in counterpoint to one another. Consequently, they can fabricate well-designed and crafted objects that have or strongly allude to a use-value, while also marketing them. Each of these three artists relates their architecture to the other elements of their practice. Pardo combines his house with the paintings, interiors and furniture he exhibits; Zittel pursues the same goals in her mobile vehicles as she does in her clothing, furniture and interiors; and Böhm maintains a distinct tension between her porch and the furniture and interiors she designs. The upshot is a carefully conceived practice that puts the notion of simultaneity into play in a different way in each case.

Kathrin Böhm with Stefan Saffer & Andreas Lang
Mobile Porch
2000

Conclusion

Ray and Charles Eames
Room Design: An Exhibition for Modern Living
1949
Eames Office

The notion of simultaneity is thus the key ingredient to design art. In spite of the prevailing fashion in art history for pushing the achievements of the Bauhaus, De Stijl and the Russian Constructivists into the spotlight, it was in fact their contemporaries such as Sonia Delaunay who moved between both professional roles and different disciplines with greater ease. Within the Bauhaus, the tight grip exerted by its exponents over exchanges between disciplines tended to straightjacket them to such an extent that all sense of intuition and excitement was squeezed out. In De Stijl the romance never seemed to quite work either, as each artist or architect staunchly policed the perimeters of his own professional territory. Van Doesburg's insistence on interpreting quandaries pertaining to the interior through painting and painting alone, and his astonishment when his proposals were turned down, reveals how inflexible he really was. Russian Constructivists such as Varvara Stepanova eventually veered away from the notion of simultaneity altogether, with the result that once she had finished exploring textile design and the political climate had changed, she returned to traditional still-life painting of all things.

Because artists such as Delaunay glided between painting and design with such consummate ease, it is easy to overlook just how radical their practice really was. In Delaunay's case this ease exudes a sense of nonchalance that conceals her insistence on precision and specificity in each of the media in which she worked. The way in which her movement between art and design energised both unmitigatedly, lends her ideas reason and pushes them beyond just

being some kind of pose – although even if that was all they were they would still be pretty enticing. Delaunay managed to be gregarious while at the same time demanding of herself an exacting sense of specificity within each of the myriad disciplines in which she worked. Certain aspects of contemporary design art are undoubtedly indebted to her.

Ray Eames moved with just as much ease between even more disciplines and roles. From the platform of design she turned her hand to sculpture – in the guise of the plywood pieces derived from the plywood splints and painting – and colourful decoration with her realisation of 'functioning decoration' for the Eames House in Pacific Palisades, California. She also pursued design in the guise of graphic work for magazine covers and advertisements, furniture with the *LCW* chair and architecture with the Eames House. That Ray and Charles used film to comment on all these interchanges and so created a new one is equally remarkable. The ingenuity that comes with this ease pervades the Eameses' practice to such an extent that it is surely inconceivable without this fluid exchange. Hence, too, their attraction for contemporary artists.

Were either Delaunay or Ray Eames to have resisted the relationship between art and design, they may have ended up more like Bridget Riley or Donald Judd. Although not necessarily a disagreeable result, this would have meant that their reach was severely limited early on. Riley may never have had any desire to dabble in design, but her practice would surely have been more racy if only she had; likewise, Judd's sulky attempts to parry with design led to a limited sense of practice. If only Judd could have either thought about his relationship with

Sonia Delaunay
Joker
1962
Centre Georges
Pompidou, Paris

EA

Sonia Delaunay 69

design more carefully, or alternatively not even thought about it at all, then his sense of a practice incorporating both art and design could have been a little more exciting.

Contemporary artists pursuing similar paths to Delaunay and Ray Eames – and Jorge Pardo and his contemporary Pae White (b. 1963) immediately come to mind – energise the art and design interchange. White is exemplary as she works as both a designer and an artist often in the same project; it is frequently not clear which hat she has on when, nor whether the outcome is 'design' or 'art', and this is probably part of the point. White thinks up advertisement schemes and book layouts for galleries, fabricates functional objects like barbecues and non-functional things like mobiles. Each project passes through the gallery system and so accrues something from it, but in each case it is something quite distinct. An advertisement that appears in a magazine and so in an edition of thousands has a precise function as well as a more imprecise aesthetic one, but she makes these functions run together. In the case of an exhibition catalogue such as the one designed for *Against Design: Art, Utility and Design* at the Kemper Museum of Art, Kansas City, 2001, not only did White design the representation of the artists in the show, she is also presented herself as an equal part of the exhibition. The only difference was that she has opted to realise her contribution through the medium of graphic design. White's mobiles and other more gallery-bound objects converge around a similar formal language to that deployed in the graphic work, and so more than any one individual piece, it is the way in which all her work interrelates that

lends her practice its dynamic character.

In order to re-tool the notion of simultaneity, Pardo revisits watershed moments in modernism and empties them of their rhetoric of purity and utopianism. Some may think that the result stems from a shrewd sense of commercialism, deftly hidden beneath the veneer of the relaxed 1970s-style loafer. They are partly mistaken, however, since behind the apparent simplicity of his work lies a keen sensibility that is receptive to each discipline and professional role with which he becomes involved, even though he by no means has an equal purchase on all of them. The incorporation of the commercial end of art making into the actual fabric of a practice without either forcing an indolent meta-critical reflection, nor falling prey to the insipidity that can result from rampant commercialism, is one of the most delectable characteristics of his practice. Pardo's former assistant, the artist Dave Muller, even comments on this with his witty watercolour, *Trade?* 2000.

Elements of the 1970s loafer are nevertheless undeniably present in Pardo and so this seems as good a time as any to conclude the references to *The Ice Storm* made in the Introduction. The logical extension of Joe Scanlan's analogies between the film and design art is to extend a more general analogy between it and one of the film's central themes, husband and wife swapping. For perhaps the exchange between art and design is, at its best, not so much a romance as this book's subtitle suggests, but more of an illicit affair. This analogy could be further extended to the cast of the film who could be said to correspond to some of the characters appearing in the chapters

Pae White
Magazine advertisement
for gallery
neugerriemschneider,
Berlin, in *Frieze*
2001

Have two pieces by Jorge Pardo from 1995, will trade for work by André Cadere.

Call Dave at 323 478-0079 or Jake at 44 20 8983 3878

Dave Muller
Trade?
2000
Blum & Poe,
Los Angeles

1 Ruskin, 1956, p.75,
2 Wilde, 'The Critic as
Artist' (1891), quoted
in Stark, 1999, p.18.

above. The first correlation to be drawn would have to be between Benjamin Hood, the film's male lead performed by Kevin Kline, and Judd. Hood snaps at the children's heels, particularly when they are trying to get into one another's pants, and attempts an affair with a neighbour but cannot really keep her satisfied and so it comes to an end. There is much to be learned from Hood's example.

Not only do Delaunay, Pardo *et al.* have in common the ease with which they deal with the exchange between disciplines and their corresponding professional roles, they also place decoration and ornamentation high on the agenda. Nowhere is the accord between certain exponents of design art and John Ruskin's writing on the subject closer than when the art historian conjectures that: 'Wherever you can rest, there decorate', for 'you must not mix ornament with business, any more than you can mix play'.[1] Ruskin is not saying that ornament is not good enough for business, but rather the exact opposite: that ornament is too good a thing to be just a background to the fast pace of the work place, and it should instead be kept for a relaxed environment. There is even the suggestion in Ruskin that if it is felicitous enough, then ornament can evince a sense of rest. Oscar Wilde extended this aspect of the debate when he declared that: 'the art that is frankly decorative is the art to live with ... It is, for all visible arts, the one art that creates in us both mood and temperament. The repetitions of pattern give us rest.'[2] In his terms, a decorative type of art most definitely affects the state of mind of the individual beholder, a desirable thing for a writer such as Wilde, who required the exuberant and ornate surroundings of

the aesthete to nurture his effervescent prose style. Another way of reading Ruskin's and Wilde's accounts of ornament from a contemporary perspective is to conjecture that ornament is good for the home, while grey conceptualism – the very art that adamantly denies a relationship with design – should be relegated to the office.

There are other artists and critics who engage with design but who have been left out of this book, and indeed it would have ended up somewhere entirely different had it taken one of them as its starting point. But who would rather spend their time contemplating a urinal instead of a chair? A chair can not only be looked at but also sat on. The same is true for the metaphorical variety provided by Matisse's paintings even if it is only the mind that can find repose there. So, despite the fact that vast ideological spaces have been traversed since Matisse made his comment about art being an armchair for the tired businessperson, its implications are still being unfolded today. At the very least, the outcome is that the beholder can now literally sit on art that they are also looking at.

Selected further reading

Reyner Banham (ed.), *The Aspen Papers: Twenty Years of Design Theory from the International Conference at Aspen*, New York and London 1974

Herbert Bayer and Walter Gropius (eds.), *Bauhaus 1919–1928*, New York 1938

Vilém Flusser, *The Shape of Things: A Philosophy of Design*, London and New York 1999

Scott Burton, 'Furniture Journal: Rietveld', *Art in America*, November 1980

Sonia Delauney, 'The Influence of Painting on Fashion Design', *The New Art of Color: The Writings of Robert and Sonia Delaunay*, ed. Arthur A. Cohen, London and New York 1978

Theo van Doesburg, *Principles of Neo-Plastic Plastic Art*, London 1969

Liam Gillick, *Liam Gillick: The Woodway*, exh. cat., Whitechapel Art Gallery, London 2002

Dan Graham, Art as Design/Design as Art', *Rock My Religion*, Cambridge, Massachusetts, and London 1993

Jessica Helfand, *Screen: Essays on Graphic Design, New Media, and Visual Culture*, New York 2001

Donald Judd, *Complete Writings 1959–1975*, Halifax, Nova Scotia 1975

Rick Moody, *The Ice Storm*, New York and London 1998

Bruno Munari, *Design As Art*, New York and London 1971

George Nelson, *George Nelson on Design*, London 1979

Paul Rand, *Thoughts on Design*, New York and London 1970

Alois Riegl, *The Late Roman Art Industry*, Rome 1985

Ed Ruscha, *Leave Any Information at the Signal: Interviews, Bits, Pages*, ed. Alexandra Schwartz, Cambridge, Massachusetts, and London 2002

Joe Scanlan and Neal Jackson, 'Please, Eat the Daisies', *Art Issues*, January/February 2001

Alison and Peter Smithson, *Ordinariness and Light: Urban Theories 1952–1960 and their Application in a Building Project 1963–1970*, London 1970

Ettore Sottsass, *Ettore Sottsass: Designer Artist Architect*, Zurich 1993

Oscar Wilde, 'The House Beautiful', *The Collins Complete Works of Oscar Wilde*, London and New York 2001

Photo credits   Copyright

Artforum 11
Bildgeman Art Library 23, 51
Cathy Carver, courtesy Dia Center for the Arts 9, 10
Scott Frances © Esto 104
Courtesy of Gagosian Gallery, London 68–9, 70, 92
John Gilliland 30
Haunch of Venison Gallery, London 118, 119, 121
Hulton Archives 46
ICN Rijswijk, Amsterdam, Donation Van Moorsel 88
Courtesy Lillian Kiesler 90
L&M Services B.V. Amsterdam 20040106 24 bottom, 25
David Lubarsky 60
Magnum/Robert R. Capa 124–5
Robert E. Mates and Paul Katz 67
Grant Mudford 108–9, 110
© Murdoch 18–9, 110
A. Newhart 52
Courtesy Catherine Prouvé 61
Courtesy Regen Projects, Los Angeles 128
© Photo SCALA 89
Courtesy Joe Scanlan 62, 63
Julius Shulman 112–13, 114–15, 122
© Ted Spiegel/CORBIS 17
Ezra Stoller © Esto 80–1, 103
Tate Photography 40–1
The Andy Warhol Museum, Pittsburgh 30
Joshua White, courtesy Blum & Poe, Los Angeles 2, 138
Woka, Vienna 77

Alvar Aalto © The artist's estate
Richard Artschwager © ARS, NY and DACS, London 2005
Kathrin Böhm © The artist
John Chamberlain © ARS, NY and DACS, London 2005
Sonia Delaunay L&M Services B.V. Amsterdam 20040106
Sam Durant © The artist
Charles and Ray Eames © 2003
Lucia Eames dba Eames Office (www.eamesoffice.com)
Todd Eberle © The artist
Sylvie Fleury © The artist
Gelatin © Gelatin
Liam Gillick © The artist
Dan Graham © The artist
Eileen Gray © The artist's estate
Richard Hamilton © Richard Hamilton 2004. All Rights Reserved, DACS
Donald Judd © The Judd Foundation
Ellsworth Kelly © The artist
Frederick Kiesler © The artist
Jim Lambie © The artist, courtesy Sadie Coles HQ, London
Andreas Lang © The artist
Henri Matisse © Succession H. Matisse/DACS 2005
Dave Muller © The artist
Takashi Murakami © 2003 Takashi Murakami/Kaikai Kiki Co., Ltd. All Rights Reserved
Kenneth Noland © Kenneth Noland/VAGA, NY/DACS, London 2005
Hélio Oiticica © Projeto Hélio Oiticica
Claes Oldenburg Copyright Claes Oldenburg and Coosjie van Bruggen

Verner Panton Courtesy Verner Panton Design, Switzerland
Jorge Pardo © The artist
Charlotte Perriand © The artist's estate
Kenneth Price © The artist
Tobias Rehberger © The artist
Aleksandr Mikhajlovich Rodchenko © DACS, London 2005
Ed Ruscha © The artist's estate
Joe Scanlan © The artist
Julius Shulman Copyright J. Paul Getty Trust. Used with permission. Julius Shulman Photography Archive, Research Library at the Getty Research Institute
Stefan Saffer © The artist
Haim Steinbach © The artist
Varvara Stepanova © DACS, London 2005
Andy Warhol © The Andy Warhol Foundation for the Visual Arts, Inc./ARS, NY and DACS, London 2005
Franz West © The artist
Pae White © The artist/neugerriemschneider, Berlin
Andrea Zittel © The artist, courtesy Sadie Coles HQ, London

Index

Index